Faith and
Reason in Islam

RELATED TITLES PUBLISHED BY ONEWORLD

Islamic Philosophy, Theology and Mysticism: A Short Introduction, Majid Fakhry, ISBN 1–85168–252–X

Muslim Women Mystics: The Life of Rabi'a and other Women Mystics in Islam, Margaret Smith, ISBN 1–85168–250–3

Averroes: His Life, Works and Influences, Majid Fakhry, ISBN 1–85168–269–4

Rumi – Past and Present, East and West: The Life, Teachings and Poetry of Jalâl al-Din Rumi, Franklin D. Lewis, ISBN 1–85168–241–7

GREAT ISLAMIC WRITINGS

Faith and Reason in Islam

Averroes' Exposition of Religious Arguments

AVERROES

Translated with footnotes, index and bibliography by
IBRAHIM Y. NAJJAR

with an introduction by
MAJID FAKHRY

ONEWORLD
OXFORD

FAITH AND REASON IN ISLAM

Oneworld Publications
(Sales and Editorial)
185 Banbury Road
Oxford OX2 7AR
England
www.oneworld-publications.com

© Ibrahim Y. Najjar 2001

All rights reserved
Copyright under Berne Convention
A CIP record for this title is available
from the British Library

ISBN 1–85168–263–5

Cover design by Design Deluxe
Typeset by LaserScript Limited, Mitcham, UK
Printed and bound in Great Britain by Bell & Bain Ltd, Glasgow

For Marina, Stephanie,
Nouri, and Sally

Contents

Preface

The modern Arabic edition of *Al-Kashf 'an Manāhij al-Adilla fī 'Aqā'id al-Milla* by Abu'l-Walīd Ibn Rushd (Averroes),[1] together with *Faṣl al-Maqāl (The Decisive Treatise)* and the short tract commonly referred to as *Al-Damimah* (*The Appendix*) constitute the trilogy that was published in 1859 by M. J. Müller and translated into German in a volume entitled *Philosophie und Theologie von Averroes*.[2] A Spanish translation of this trilogy was published by M. Alonso in 1947 as *Teologia de Averroes*, Madrid-Granada.

The Müller edition was reprinted many times in Cairo, but more recently a critical edition of *Al-Kashf* was published in Cairo in 1964 by Mahmud Qasim, upon which the present English translation is based.[3] The manuscript that Qasim used is the one found in the Escorial library, number 632; it is older and more complete than the other existing manuscripts. However, reference is made to these other manuscripts in the footnotes to reflect important variations, additions, deletions,

---

1. It should be noted that Ibn Rushd is the anglicized Arabic form and Averroes the western European.
2. M. J. Müller (ed.), *Philosophie und Theologie von Averroes* (Munich: 1859), and M. J. Müller (trans.), *Philosophie und Theologie von Averroes* (Munich: Ausdem Nachlosse desselben hrsg. von der königl. Bayer. Akademie der Wissenschaften, 1875).
3. Mahmud Qasim (ed.) *Manāhij al-Adilla fī 'Aqā'id al-Milla*, 2nd edn., published in Series of Philosophical and Moral Studies. (Cairo: the Anglo-Egyptian Library, 1964). The pages of this edition are indicated in the margins of the following translation to make it easier for the reader to refer to or consult it.

alterations etc. This manuscript is dated 724H[4] and written in a clear Andalusian hand. It is referred to here as manuscript "S".[5]

Manuscript number 129 is found in the Taymuria library in the House of Egyptian Books and is referred to here in the footnotes as "A". It is dated 1202H. and written in an elegant Ottoman hand, but is itself copied from an earlier version written by Abdullah Ibn Uthman in 1135H. However, many pages in it are missing. Manuscript number 133, found also in the Taymuria library, is referred to as "B". This is written in a Maghribi hand, but is undated, though it seems more recent than the previous one and considerably more accurate. The copy of *Manāhij* which was published by M. J. Müller under the title *Philosophie und Theologie Von Averroes* in 1859 is referred to here as Müller.

Ibn Rushd cites verses from the Qur'an without giving their numbers. The reader is supplied with verse numbers and an index. Majid Fakhry's modern translation of the Qur'an is used as reference.[6]

As mentioned earlier, *Al-Kashf*, together with *Faṣl al-Maqāl* [7] and *al-Ḍamima*, constitute Ibn Rushd's trilogy, and when George Hourani translated *Faṣl al-Maqāl* into English as *On the Harmony of Religion and Philosophy*,[8] he translated a small part of chapter nine and chapter ten of *Al-Kashf*.

Isb Rushd's *Exposition of Religious Arguments* contains sufficient evidence to motivate the reader to re-examine many popular views about Ibn Rushd. I will briefly draw the attention of the reader to some of the issues

---

4. "H" following the date refers to Hegira, the emigration of the Prophet Muḥammad and his followers from Mecca to Medina in 622 C.E., which constitutes the first year of the Hegira calendar.

5. As my translation was being reviewed for publication, a new critical edition of the Escorial manuscript appeared by Mustapha Hanafi, with an introduction by Muḥammad 'Abid Al-Jabiri and published by the Center of Studies for Arab Unity, Markaz Dirāsāt al-Wahda al-'Arabia, Beirut, 1998.

6. The Qur'an: *A Modern English Version* Majid Fakhry (trans.), (Reading: Garnet Publishing, 1997). Other translations of the Qur'an have been consulted, particularly that of Arthur J. Arberry, *The Koran Interpreted*, (London: Oxford University Press, 1964). Other works consulted as reference are: M. Fakhry, *A History of Islamic Philosophy*, M.C. Hernandez, *Ibn Rushd (Averroes)*; L. Gauthier, *Ibn Roshd (Averroes)*; M. Marakushi, *Al-Mū'jib fi Akhbār al-Maghrib*, and E. Renan, *Averroes et l'averroïsme*.

7. George Hourani (ed.), *Kitāb Faṣl al-Maqāl* (Leiden: E. J. Brill, 1959).

8. George Hourani (trans.), *On the Harmony of Religion and Philosophy* (London: Messrs. Luzac & Co., 1961).

in the book where such a re-examination is called for. Some believe that Averroes is an Aristotelian rationalist who was bent on undermining or subverting religion, albeit while upholding the harmony between religion and philosophy or faith and reason. It is also believed that having accepted the Aristotelian metaphysics and the place of the Unmoved Mover in it Ibn Rushd could not believe in the creation of the world, revealed religions and the hereafter. The reader of *The Exposition*, however, will be surprised to find Ibn Rushd offering one argument after another in support of a different position. While maintaining the harmony between religion and philosophy, Averroes shows that neither discipline is in need of subverting the other. They are both legitimate human endeavors with clear lines of demarcation. They work in harmony with each other rather than in conflict. This is evident in the crucial issue of the separation between clear religious texts and vague or ambiguous ones. While no disagreement arises about clear religious texts and their acceptance is required of all believers upon faith, ambiguous texts call for interpretation and the interference of reason. One obvious requirement is that interpretations cannot come into conflict with clear and unambiguous texts. Reason is necessary, and without it the understanding of religious texts remains incomplete.

Another issue dealt with in *The Exposition* is the central belief in the existence of God and the related problem of the creation of the world. Ibn Rushd's position on both counts is clear and his arguments are quite elaborate, simple and straightforward. He takes the theologians to task, especially the Ash'arites, scrutinizing their arguments and maintaining that their attempt to prove the creation of the world is flawed. He distinguishes two proofs offered by this school: the first is adhered to by the majority of this group and the second is held by Abū al-Ma'ali al-Juwayni, the illustrious teacher of Abū Ḥāmid al-Ghazāli. The first argument rests on three premises: that substances are always found inseparable from accidents, that accidents are created; and that what cannot exist separately from created accidents is itself created. The crux of Averroes' criticism of this argument is that it fails to apply to the world as a whole, even though it might apply to individual substances in it. As far as Abū al-Ma'āli's argument is concerned, it is based on two premises:

that the world with everything in it is contingent, i.e., it could have been other than what it is, and that whatever is contingent is created. Ibn Rushd rejects this argument, pointing to its Avicennian origins and maintaining that its first premise is merely rhetorical and factually incorrect, and that its second premise is not demonstrable; the two great philosophers Plato and Aristotle took opposite views regarding it. Abū al-Maʿālī's proof misses its point; instead of pointing to the wise creator of the world, it repudiates the principles of causality, thus abandoning the world to the vagaries of coincidence.

According to Ibn Rushd, there are two arguments that prove the existence of God and that everyone accepts: the argument from invention, *Dalil al-Ikhtira'* and the argument from design, *Dalil al-'Inaya*. Observation shows that everything in the world is ordered according to a fixed causal pattern which is conducive to serving the universal goal of the existence and well-being of mankind, as the Qur'an itself asserts in a series of verses. Likewise, observation, supported by many verses in the Qur'an, shows that there are created or invented substances in the world, like the coming of life out of inanimate objects and the creation of sensations and cognitions. The Precious Book (the Qur'an) also contains many verses that refer to the two arguments combined. Averroes maintains that when rational beings find objects in nature possessing the definite characteristics referred to by these two arguments – namely the utility and purposefulness of their parts to human purposes – they infer the existence of a wise Maker or manufacturer behind them. Similarly, when one contemplates the world with its existing entities and sees how well they are ordered and causally related, and observes their conduciveness to life and the well-being of mankind, it becomes rather impossible not to attribute the existence of the world to a wise Maker who is God. Ibn Rushd does not believe that there are deductive arguments that can prove the existence of God, but his two inductive arguments are the only arguments the human mind is capable of offering to prove the existence of God. Chapter one and the first part of chapter five of this translation offer a full discussion of these two arguments.

As for the widespread belief that Averroes held a position maintaining the superiority of philosophers to the ordinary people and the dialectic theologians, Ibn Rushd provides a detailed argument to show that in *The Exposition* he does not subscribe to this position. All people, he maintains, are equal in their rationality and capacity for understanding. Where they differ is in the degree to which they are prepared to deal with highly abstract issues and detailed arguments that could not be understood except after a long period of arduous study. Unlike the common people and the theologians, the philosophers take the needed time and acquire the appropriate skills for understanding such arguments. What sets the philosophers apart is not the superiority of their intellect and innate competence, but rather their preoccupation with such matters over a long period of time. Philosophers are experts in their field like physicians in the field of health; the common people and the theologians are like patients who receive treatment and follow the advice of the expert doctors. The philosophers differ from other people in the degree and detail of their knowledge, but not in intellectual ability. The concluding part of chapter one offers support for this position.

On the issue of life after death, Ibn Rushd's discussion in section five of chapter five is very interesting, but basically he holds it upon faith, allowing himself to speculate only on the manner in which people survive after death. His discussion of God's attributes in chapter three is refreshing and the theory that he proposes for understanding religious texts is illuminating. Particular attention should be given to Ibn Rushd's discussions of God's unity in chapter two and God's justice in section four of chapter five.

It is quite fitting to end this Preface with a word of thanks to all those who directly or indirectly helped make this project a reality. I thank Professor Majid Fakhry for setting this translation on the right course, checking it thoroughly, and writing the Introduction. Not only did he encourage me to translate *Al-Kashf*, he continued to offer his unwavering support until seeing it published. I thank also the American University of Beirut Research Board (U.R.B.) for providing me with research grants for 1997 and 1998. As for the University of Sharjah, my present intellectual domicile, it has my sincere thanks for encouraging the publication of this translation and supporting my research. I am especially thankful to Dr. Abdul-Hamid Hallab and Dr. George K. Najjar for offering me the chance to become part of this burgeoning and forward-looking institution founded by His Highness Sheikh Dr. Sultan Bin Mohammed Al-Qasimi, the Ruler of Sharjah, whose vision led to the construction of such a magnificent edifice dedicated to the pursuit of knowledge and cultural harmony. In its promotion of dialogue and inter-cultural harmony, *The Exposition* is one of the great works in our cultural heritage that echoes His Highness's concerns and mission.

My wife, Salwa Ghaly, oversaw the whole project from its inception. To her go my sincere appreciation and thanks. As for my children, their love made the long hours of work more enjoyable. Stephanie is eight years old now, but her early curiosity about Ibn Rushd tickles my imagination. I hope that my other children Marina and Nouri and future generations will continue to find inspiration in Ibn Rushd's works.

Ibrahim Y. Najjar
University of Sharjah
September 2000

Introduction

I

Abū'l-Walīd Ibn Rushd, known in European sources as Averroes, was born in Cordova, Spain, in 1126 C.E. He studied Arabic letters (*Adab*), jurisprudence (*Fiqh*), *Kalam*, medicine and philosophy with a number of teachers, some of whose names are given in the sources. In 1169, he was introduced to the Caliph, Abū Ya'qub Yūsuf, by Ibn Tufayl (d.1185), the leading philosopher of the period and court physician to the Caliph. Abū Ya'qub Yūsuf was an avid reader of Aristotle, we are told, but complained of his "intractable and abstruse idiom". As a result of this meeting, Averroes was asked to expound the works of Aristotle for the use of the Caliph and was appointed religious judge (*qādi*) of Seville and shortly after chief judge of Cordova. In 1182, he was appointed physician royal at the court of Marrakech.

Upon the succession of the Caliph's son, nicknamed Al-Manṣūr, Averroes continued to enjoy the royal patronage, but in 1195, yielding to public pressure, the Caliph ordered the books of Averroes to be burnt, on an undefined charge of irreligion or heresy, and the teaching of philosophy and the sciences was banned, with the exception of astronomy, medicine, and arithmetic. In the same year Averroes was exiled to Lucena, to the southeast of Cordova; though shortly after he was restored to favor. In 1198, he died in Cordova at the age of seventy-two.

Averroes' writings on philosophy, jurisprudence, theology, and medicine, which have all survived in Arabic or Hebrew and Latin translations, place him in the forefront of writers on these subjects in the world of medieval Islam and beyond. He was recognized in Western Europe, starting with the thirteenth century, which witnessed the translation of his commentaries on Aristotle, as *The Commentator,* or as Dante has put it, *che gran commento feo.* These Latin translations early in that century caused a genuine intellectual stir in learned circles and laid the ground for the rise of Latin Scholasticism, one of the glories of European thought in the later Middle Ages. However, apart from his contribution to Aristotelian scholarship, which was almost unmatched until modern times, Averroes has dealt more thoroughly than any other Muslim philosopher with theological questions, including the perennial question of the relation of faith and reason, which became the pivotal issue in the Scholastic disputations of the thirteenth century and beyond in Western Europe. His contribution to those disputations is embodied in three theological treatises: *The Decisive Treatise* (*Faṣl al-Maqāl*), written in 1179; *The Exposition of the Methods of Proof* (*Al-Kashf 'an Manāhij Al-Adilla*), written in the same year; and a short tract dealing with the question of God's eternal and unchanging knowledge of particulars or contingent entities. To this trilogy should be added his systematic rebuttal of Al-Ghazāli's onslaught on Islamic Neoplatonism in the *Incoherence of the Philosophers* (*Tahāfut al-Falāsifah*), written in 1195 and entitled the *Incoherence of the Incoherence* (*Tahāfut al-Tahāfut*).

In the first of these works, *The Decisive Treatise,* Averroes sets out the appropriate methodology for the solution of the problem of the relation of religion (*sharī'a*) and philosophy (*ḥikmah*), and more specifically the way in which philosophical or logical methods of reasoning can be used in religious controversies, or applied to the interpretation of the texts of Scripture (*Shar'*). He begins by defining philosophy as "The investigation of existing entities in so far as they point to the Maker; I mean, in so far as they are made, since existing entities exhibit the Maker." It follows, he goes on to argue, that the study of philosophy is indeed recommended by the religious law (*Shar'*), as appears from a number of Qur'anic verses, such as 59: 2, which urges "people of understanding to reflect" and verse

7: 184, which asks: "Have they not considered the Kingdom of the heavens and the earth and all the things God has created?" For surely, Averroes asserts, reflection and consideration are forms of logical reasoning or deduction (*qiyās*), or "the extraction of the unknown from the known". He then proceeds to rebut the claim of the literalists and traditionalists that the use of deduction, which the first generation of Muslim scholars have shunned, is an "innovation"on the ground that juridical deduction, which is analogous to logical deduction, was subsequently practiced by the next generation and was regarded as perfectly legitimate.

Next, Averroes proceeds to ask whether "demonstration" (*burhān*), which is the highest form of logical deduction, is compatible with the explicit or implicit prescriptions of Scripture (*Shar'*). His answer is that, like the jurist who draws out or deduces his legal decisions from the sacred texts by recourse to interpretation (*ta'wīl*), the philosopher is perfectly justified in resorting to interpretation in his attempt to elicit, by means of rational deduction, the nature of reality and the way in which it leads to the knowledge of the Maker. He then defines interpretation as "the act of eliciting the real connotation of (Scriptural) terms from their figurative connotation without violating the rules of the Arabic language". However, it should be noted that not all the texts of Scripture (i.e. the Qur'an) admit of interpretation; only those parts of it which the Qur'an itself has designated as "ambiguous" (*mutashābihat*), as against those parts which it has designated as "sound" or unambiguous (*muḥkamāt*) in verses 3: 5–7. With respect to the former the Qur'an stipulates that their interpretation is imperative, but "only God and those well-grounded in knowledge" are qualified to interpret it. By those "well-grounded in knowledge", Averroes is categorical, only the philosophers or "people of demonstration" are intended, followed, in the order of their aptitudes to understand the intent of Scripture, by the "dialectical' class (or the Mutakallimun), and the "rhetorical" class (or the public at large). This threefold division of mankind is confirmed, according to Averroes, by the Qur'an itself which states in verse 16: 125, addressing the Prophet: "Call to the way of your Lord with wisdom and mild exhortation and argue with them in the best manner."

II

The second treatise, or *Exposition* (*al-Kashf*) gives, as a sequel to this methodology, a substantive statement of those articles of faith which are essential for salvation, or as Averroes puts it, "without which the faith (of the Muslim believer) is not complete". This statement, which is reminiscent of similar statements found in Medieval Scholastic treatises, such as St. Thomas Aquinas's *Summa Theologica*, opens with a chapter on the demonstration of God's existence, followed by a discussion of God's unity, His attributes and His transcendence or freedom from imperfection. This first part is then followed by a discussion of divine actions, which include the creation of the world, the commissioning of Messengers, the meaning of the divine decree and predestination, divine justice, and the nature of resurrection. The book closes with a discussion of the rules of interpretation, which had been at the center of the first volume or *The Decisive Treatise*, already discussed. Here Averroes reiterates his thesis that the statements of Scripture are either explicit, and hence do not call for any interpretation, or ambiguous and hence should be interpreted exclusively by the learned, or "those well-grounded in knowledge", as the Qur'an has put it. However, this interpretation should not be divulged to the general public, who are not able to fathom its meaning.

Earlier in *The Exposition* Averroes had argued that none of the Muslim sects, whether the literalists, the Ash'arites, the Mu'tazilites or the Esoterics (i.e. the Sufis), who accuse each other of innovation or heresy, are found upon close scrutiny to have conformed, in their interpretations or claims, to the intent of the lawgiver (the Prophet) and are therefore all guilty of innovation or heresy. This leads him to undertake at the outset to draw up a list of those articles of faith which are not open to question and to define the rules of sound interpretation.

The first rule is that none of the Islamic sects mentioned above is competent to formulate the principles of sound interpretation; only the philosophers or the learned are. The second rule is that Scripture, which addresses the three classes of men, the learned, the theologians and the common people, actually uses the three corresponding methods of proof, the demonstrative, the dialectical, and the rhetorical, to ensure that the intention of the lawgiver is understood by them all. The third rule is that interpretation should be properly understood or applied. According to Averroes, false interpretations are at the root of the rise of heretical sects in Islam, totaling, according to a Prophetic tradition (*Hadith* 72), of which only one was destined to be saved.

The line of demarcation between those parts of Scripture which may and those parts which may not be interpreted and should be accepted by the masses or common people at their face value, is clearly drawn by Averroes. It is evident from his various statements in *The Exposition* and elsewhere that interpretation is to be sought; firstly, in those cases which have not been the object of consensus (*ijma'*) by the community; secondly, where the statements of Scripture appear to be in conflict with each other; and thirdly, where those statements appear to be in conflict with the principles of philosophy or natural reason. Averroes, who was committed to the complete harmony of religious and philosophical truth, proceeds next to set forth the principal propositions around which consensus can be achieved without violating any rational or philosophical precepts, and which can be regarded as constituting the substance of an acceptable Islamic Credo, so to speak.

The list begins with those propositions that purport to demonstrate the existence of God and his unity. Here Averroes reviews and then rejects the favorite arguments of the Mutakallimun, including the Ash'arites, which rest upon the premise of the temporality of the universe (*hudūth*). This argument which goes back to the philosopher al-Kindi (d.*c*.866), who was known for his Mu'tazilite sympathies, and beyond him to John Philoponus, known in the Arabic sources as the Grammarian (d.586), states that the world, being created in time (*hādith* or *mūhdath*) must have a Creator or Originator (*Mūhdith*) who created it in time. The first premise of this argument, as Averroes observes, is supposed to be the corollary of the thesis generally adhered to by the Mutakallimun that the world is made up of indivisible particles or atoms, which by nature are evanescent. However, this thesis, according to him, is far from being demonstrable in a manner accessible to the general public or even skilled logicians. The second argument, favored by the Ash'arites, as propounded

by al-Juwayni (d.1086), Al-Ghazāli's illustrious teacher, is the argument
from contingency, which Avicenna (d.1037) himself had adumbrated. It
states that the world's being contingent (*jā'iz* or *mūmkin*) requires that
there be a determinant who is not contingent, whom Avicenna designated
the Necessary Being. Averroes rejects this argument on the ground that
the major premise, the contingency of the world, is purely rhetorical and
rests on the repudiation of the universal principle of causality, which
entails that the world is causally ordered in a way which manifests the
wisdom of its Creator. Thus, whoever repudiates this principle, not only
repudiates that wisdom, but is unable in fact to offer a coherent proof of
God's existence. He is, consequently, forced to concede that the world is
the product of the blind forces of chance, or simply random (*'Ittifāq*).

Significantly, Averroes proposes two alternative proofs for the
existence of God, that of providence and that of invention, to both of
which "the Precious Book" (the Qur'an) has drawn attention, as he puts it,
in a variety of verses. The former rests on the premise that all existing
entities here below have come to exist in order to subserve the interests of
mankind and for this reason are necessarily due to a willing and intending
Agent and cannot be the product of chance. The other argument rests on
the premise that everything in the world is "invented" or made by an
Inventor or Maker, who is God. Averroes then goes on to argue that the
knowledge of God as Inventor or Maker of the world is not possible,
unless one knows "the reality of things, whereby the reality of invention
exhibited in all existing entities is revealed to him".

III

With respect to the attributes of God, explicitly given in the "Precious
Book", they are in fact the so-called seven attributes of perfection found
in man; namely, life, knowledge, power, will, hearing, sight, and speech,
which attributes the Mutakallimun, whether Mu'tazilites or Ash'arites,
actually concurred in. However, Averroes disagrees with both sects
regarding the mode of predicating them of God. Thus the Ash'arites hold
that the attributes of knowledge and will are eternal, adding that God
knows created entities by means of an eternal knowledge and wills them

by means of an eternal will. Both notions, according to Averroes, are logically absurd. For knowledge is consequent on the existence of its object and so is will. It follows that God knows an entity when it comes to exist or ceases to exist as He wills it to exist or to cease to exist. To contend that God knows and wills entities created in time by means of an eternal knowledge and will leaves unexplained the lapse of time intervening between God's will to create an entity in time and its actual coming to exist in time, in the light of God's infinite power. The explicit teaching of Scripture, according to Averroes, is simply that created entities are known to God and willed by Him at the very moment He wishes them to exist; it does not determine whether such knowing and willing are temporal or eternal. Such knowledge and will are entirely different from our own and the mode of predicating them of God is unknown to us, as he has stated in *The Incoherence*. In *The Decisive Treatise* and *The Appendix* he states that God's knowledge of the object is the *cause* of that object, whereas our knowledge is the *effect* of the object.

As for speech, around which controversy raged for centuries between the Mu'tazilites, who held that God's speech, as embodied in the Qur'an, is created or temporal, and the Ḥanbalites and the Ash'arites, who believed it to be uncreated or eternal, Averroes' position is that speech is the corollary of knowledge and action. God, as the supreme Knower and Maker, must be capable of speech, and this speech is revealed to mankind through the prophets, either directly or indirectly through the intermediation of angels. However, there is an additional part of God's speech, which "He communicates to the learned, who are the heirs of the prophets in the form of demonstrative knowledge," by which Averroes undoubtedly meant the highest form of philosophical discourse. On the question of the status of the Qur'an, which is God's speech, Averroes distinguishes between the meanings of the words denoting this speech and the words we use in speech; the former are created by God, the latter are our own work, "by God's leave".

With respect to the two attributes of hearing and seeing, Averroes takes the line that God must possess those two attributes, by reason of the fact that hearing and sight bear on "certain apprehended properties which pertain to existing entities, but are not apprehended by reason". God, being the Creator or Maker of these entities must be capable of knowing everything pertaining to them and must, accordingly, possess the two attributes of hearing and sight, whereby they are thoroughly known, not only as objects of thought, but as objects of sense, as well.

IV

The first part of *The Exposition*, as we have seen, deals with God's existence and his attributes, or *de Deo Uno*, as the Medieval Latin Scholastic treatises have it; the second part deals with His actions. Under this rubric, Averroes deals with five questions: the creation of the world, the commissioning of prophets, divine justice, the divine decree, and resurrection.

With respect to the first question, Averroes inveighs against the Ash'arite methods of proving that the world is the creation of God on the grounds that they are neither demonstrative, nor suited to the learned, "common", or general public, since they base those proofs on complex premises which confuse, rather than instruct the latter, and fall short of the criteria of demonstration laid down by the former. The method Scripture itself has adopted is actually the simple method commonly agreed and resting on the principle of providence. The crux of this method is the observation that everything in the world is ordered according to a fixed causal pattern which is conducive to serving the universal goal of the existence and well-being of mankind, as the Qur'an itself asserts in a series of verses. By repudiating the principle of causality, as we have seen, the Ash'arites have abandoned the world to the vagaries of chance and cast doubt on divine wisdom, which is revealed in this orderly pattern and is the key to demonstrating the existence of its Author.

The question of the duration of the world, which was at the center of Al-Ghazāli's attack on the Muslim Neoplatonists Al-Farabi and Avicenna, and beyond them Aristotle, gives Averroes the opportunity to counter Al-Ghazāli's arguments and reassert Aristotle's thesis that the world is eternal and indestructible. In *The Decisive Treatise*, he argues that the differences between Al-Ghazāli and the Ash'arites, on the one hand, and "the ancient philosophers", with Aristotle at their head, on the other, are purely semantic, and are not so divergent as to justify the charges of irreligion

(*Kufr*) leveled at the philosophers by Al-Ghazāli. In fact, the Ash'arites, contrary to their allegations, cannot produce a single Qur'anic verse in support of their thesis that the world has a beginning in time. Rather the contrary, many Qur'anic verses appear to assert that "the form the world is created in reality, but its existence and temporal duration are continuous *a parte ante* and *a parte post*". Thus, verse 11: 7, which states that "it is He who created the heavens and the earth, while His Throne rested on water", implies on the surface of it that the Throne, water, and the time which measures their duration existed prior to the moment of creation. Similarly, verse 41: 11, which states: "Then he arose to heaven which consisted of smoke", implies that the heaven was created from something already existing, which is smoke.[1]

In *The Exposition*, Averroes justifies the use of such language on the ground that Scripture, in its attempt to instruct the common people, has resorted to the method of "sensuous representation" accessible to them, since creation out of nothing and in no time is something which the common people, and even the learned, are unable to grasp. In such cases it is the duty of the learned to interpret such representations; that of the common people to accept them at their face value. Averroes, who never in fact abandoned the Aristotelian thesis of an eternal universe, whilst willing to entertain the Islamic concept of a created universe, believed it necessary to distinguish between continuous (*dā'im*) and discontinuous (*munqati'*) creation, as he has put it in *The Incoherence*. The former, the eternal creation is certainly more appropriate where the actions of the Omnipotent Creator are concerned, since it is inconceivable that an interval or lapse of time should intervene between His willing and His action, as is the case with finite agents.

V

On the question of commissioning prophets or divine Messengers to mankind and the probative grounds of authenticating their claims to be genuine Messengers or emissaries of God, Averroes is critical of the

---

1. Cf. *Faṣl al-Maqāl*. Ed. Muhammad 'Abed Al Jabiri, Beirut: Center for Studies on Arab Unity, 1997, p.106, section 41.

Ash'arite thesis that miracle is an essential warrant of the truthfulness of prophetic claims. The Qur'an itself, he argues, confirms this point, as appears from those verses in which the Prophet is said to have declined to meet the challenge of his hearers "to cause springs to gush out from the ground for us" (Qur'an 17: 90), on the ground that he "was nothing other than a human messenger" (17: 93). This is confirmed by God's own refusal, in verse 17: 60, to send down miraculous "signs" to sway the unbelievers. The only miracle the Prophet resorted to in summoning mankind to believe in his message was "the Precious Book" whose miraculousness is affirmed in such verses as 17: 89, which challenges men and *jinn* to come up "with the like of this Qur'an", without any prospect of success, "even if they were to back one another up".

The evidence for the miraculousness of the Qur'an is then given by Averroes as follows. First, the theoretical and practical prescriptions which it has laid down are not the product of human ingenuity, but rather of divine revelation, especially since the Prophet who transmitted them to mankind was illiterate. Compared to the prescriptions embodied in the Scriptures of Jews and Christians, those of the Qur'an are far superior. Secondly, the prognostications embodied in the Qur'an confirm the Prophet's claims. (Significantly, Averroes does not give any instances of those prognostications, unlike the majority of the commentators and biographers of the Prophet.) Thirdly, the Qur'an's literary excellence sets it apart from any product of the pen of the greatest Arab literary masters and cannot for that reason be the product of human deliberation or reflection. Averroes, then, concludes the discussion of miracles by comparing the miracles attributed to Jesus and other 'divine messengers', such as Moses, to the Qur'an, Muḥammad's greatest miracle. For him, the miraculousness of the former is *extrinsic*, whereas that of the latter is *intrinsic*, and this proves conclusively that it is superior.

The third and fourth questions of the second part of *The Exposition* deal with two related issues of moral theology, predestination and divine justice. With respect to the first question, Averroes rightly observes that the evidence of Scripture (*Shar'*) is found upon close scrutiny to be conflicting. Thus we find in both the Qur'an and the

Traditions of the Prophet statements which appear to support free will or acquisition (*iktisāb, kasb*) and its opposite. This has led to the rise of three rival sects; the Mu'tazilites, who support free will; the Determinists, who deny it; and the Ash'arites, who tried to mediate between the two parties and introduced in the process the concept of "acquisition". What is more, observes Averroes, even the evidence of reason appears to be conflicting, due to the diametrically opposed arguments which can be advanced in support of both free will and predestination. Thus determinism (*jabr*) may be criticized on the ground that it renders religious obligation meaningless and any provision for the morrow, in the expectation of bringing about certain advantages and warding off certain disadvantages, entirely irrational. This in turn would render all human arts and crafts futile. To reconcile the two views, as Scripture itself appears to demand, we should understand, as Averroes argues, that human actions are the product of those internal faculties which God has implanted in us *as well as* those external forces which allow for the realization of our deliberately chosen aims. It is because those forces operate in accordance with a thoroughly rigorous causal pattern which God has imposed on the whole natural order, and which is in fact synonymous with the "Preserved Tablet" or the divine decree, that our own actions become possible and accord with our own deliberation and choice.

In defending the principle of causality against the attacks of Al-Ghazālī and the Ash'arites in general, who held that this principle conflicts with the consensus of Muslims that God is the Sole Agent, and accordingly is at liberty to act freely and miraculously in the world, Averroes argues that the term "agent" admits of two senses, real and figurative. God is indeed the real and ultimate Agent, who operates by means of those figurative, secondary agents or causes that He not only creates, but preserves in existence. This is confirmed by both reason and observation. For, but for the specific natures and properties pertaining to existing entities as we know them, on the one hand, and the influence of external, physical agencies, such as the stars, wind, rain, and sea, on the other, it would not be possible for plants, animals or humans to subsist, let alone to act effectively in the world. The Qur'an itself confirms this, in those verses which speak of God "subjecting day and night, the sun and the moon and whatever is in heavens and on earth to mankind" (Qur'an 28: 73; 45: 12; 14: 33) as an instance of His mercy.

For all these reasons, Averroes concludes that neither the Mu'tazilite (or libertarian) position nor the Hanbalite (or deterministic) position is tenable. The Ash'arite position, which purports to mediate between the two positions, is meaningless. For it rests almost exclusively on the alleged difference between the voluntary movement of the hand, which they call acquired or free, and the compulsory movement of convulsion. However, since neither movement, according to them, is due to us, but rather to God, the difference between the two movements turns out to be semantic or even fictitious; it does not contribute in the least to the solution of the problem of free will or acquisition.

With respect to divine justice, the Ash'arites, according to Averroes, have taken the position which is "repugnant to both reason and religion", that justice and injustice are entirely dependent on divine commands and prohibitions, so that no action is just or unjust in itself. It follows on this view that the worst sins, such as blasphemy or disobeying God's orders, would have been just had God commanded them. The Qur'an itself, however, has asserted repeatedly that "God is not unjust to his servants" (verses 8: 53; 22: 10 etc.) and elsewhere that "Surely, God is not unjust to people, but people are unjust to themselves" (10: 45).

Averroes next examines the arguments advanced by the Ash'arites in support of their view that God is entirely at liberty to do what He pleases. They refer to the statements in the Qur'an which speak of God leading astray and guiding aright. Those statements, he argues, should not be taken at face value, because they are contradicted by those other verses, such as verse 39: 9, which asserts, that "God does not approve of disbelief in his servants", and hence will not lead them astray. The right interpretation of the verses which speak of God leading astray or guiding aright is that they refer to "His prior will which stipulated that there shall exist among the innumerable variety of existing entities some wayward people; I mean, some who are disposed by their own natures to go astray, and that they are driven thereto by what surrounds them of internal and external causes that lead them astray" see p. 117. Thus the responsibility for leading people astray is not God's, but rather their own natures, the external causes operating on them or the two together.

Averroes does not question the thesis that God is the Creator of both good and evil; he simply argues that this thesis should be properly understood. God, in fact, creates the good for its own sake, *whereas He creates evil for the sake of the good* that may ensue upon it, so that His creating evil cannot be said to be unjust. Add to this the fact that if we compare the evil ensuing upon the creation of a certain entity, such as fire, with the parallel good, we will find that the good is definitely preponderant. The common people should be urged to accept the view that God creates both good and evil at its face value, lest they should question the measure of God's power and in particular whether He is capable of creating that which is absolutely good or free from evil. That possibility is, for Averroes, logically foreclosed, since the creation of the absolutely good, or God's equal, is logically impossible.

VI

The last substantive question dealt with in *The Exposition* is that of resurrection or survival after death (*ma'ād*), which had been at the center of the controversy between the philosophers and the Mutakallimun from the earliest times and which Al-Ghazāli regarded as the third grievous error of the philosophers, especially those, like Avicenna, who stopped short of bodily resurrection. For Averroes, survival after death is something upon whose reality all religious scriptures are in accord with the demonstrations of the learned. The various religious scriptures, however, disagree regarding the *mode* of such survival. Some have regarded it as spiritual, pertaining to the soul only; others to both soul and body. However, the difference between the various scriptures turns on the kind of "representations" they resort to in speaking of the fate of the soul after death, which in perfect agreement with the philosophers, they all regard as immortal. Thus, some religious creeds represent the pleasures and pains in store for the soul in the hereafter in gross sensuous terms, such as the Garden and Hellfire, because such representations are more effective in compelling the assent of the general public, as is the case with "this our own religion, which is Islam". Other religions (presumably Christianity) resort to "spiritual representations", which are less effective in compelling the assent of the common people.

Averroes proceeds next to distinguish three categories of Muslim sects, regarding the mode of survival after death. (1) Some Muslims, he observes, have held that the mode of man's existence in the hereafter is identical with his existence in this world with one difference; namely, that the former is permanent, while the latter is ephemeral; (2) others have held that the mode of man's existence in the afterlife is spiritual, as the Sufis have held; (3) still others have held that the corporeal existence of mankind in the hereafter is different from the corporeality of the present life.

The last view appears to be the one with which Averroes is in sympathy and is characterized by him as the one appropriate to the élite; that is, the philosophers. It is absurd, he argues, that the same body which has disintegrated at death and turned into dust; which changed into a vegetable, which was consumed by a male, and subsequently turned into semen, which gave rise to an infant, can be resurrected unchanged after death. It is more reasonable to assume that the resurrected body is analogous to, rather than identical with, the terrestrial body. Averroes concedes, in conclusion, that the obligation incumbent on the believer is to assent to that mode of resurrection commensurate with his under-standing, so long as he does not question the *fact* of resurrection, or as he consistently says, survival after death (*ma'ād*). This survival, he adds, is confirmed by the Qur'an which speaks in verse 39: 43 of the "death of the soul" as something analogous to sleep. What is corrupted in both cases is actually the organ or instrument (*ālah*), not the soul itself. He even compares this view to Aristotle's statement in *De Anima* (408 b21), that were the old man given an eye similar to that of the young man, he would be able to see just as well as the young man. The inference here appears to be that the body is to the soul what the instrument or organ is to its user, as Plato had actually held. Aristotle himself had struggled hard in *De Anima* to rid himself of this view of his master.

As mentioned earlier, the whole treatise closes with an appendix "On the Canon of Interpretation", in which Averroes lists the cases in which interpretation of scriptural passages is permissible and those in which it is not. He inveighs in this connection against those, who like Al-Ghazāli, were unwilling to recognize this distinction and consequently the class of people to whom those interpretations may be divulged. The result has been that they led the common people astray and contributed to the rise of sectarian strife in Islam. He expresses the wish at this point to have the opportunity "to discuss the totality of the statements of Scripture and elicit in the process what should be interpreted or not, and if interpreted, to whom (such interpretation) should be addressed; I mean, regarding those passages of the Qur'an and the traditions of the prophet [Hadith]" (see p. 131).

Averroes never fulfilled this wish, as far as we know, but *The Exposition* stands out nonetheless as a remarkable instance of his judicious and rigorous application of the method of interpretation and remains unparalleled in the whole history of Islam. Of his predecessors, only Al-Kindi (d.*c*.866) comes closest to shouldering this task of scriptural interpretation, upon which the Ḥanbalites, the Malikites, and, to a lesser extent, the Ash'arites had frowned. Al-Kindi's performance in that respect, at least as far as those of his works which have reached us are concerned, pales into insignificance when compared to this determined effort of Averroes to apply the canons of rational discourse to the problematic or ambiguous passages of Scripture.

Majid Fakhry

1

On proving God's existence

132 In the name of God, the Compassionate, the Merciful, O God our Lord, we ask Your assistance, and prayers and greetings be upon our Master Muḥammad and his family.

Thus spoke the jurist, the learned and unique scholar Abū'l-Walīd Muḥammad Ibn Aḥmad Ibn Muḥammad Ibn Aḥmad Ibn Rushd, may God be pleased with him and bless him with His benevolence.

We praise God who has favored those whom He pleased (to favor) with His wisdom, leading them to understand His religion[1] and follow His path, and revealing to them, from His hidden knowledge the meaning of His revelation and the intent of the message of His Prophet to mankind, that which exposed to them the deviation of those who strayed from the path of His religion, as well as the distortion of the disbelievers among His Community. It was also exposed to them that there are interpretations that God and His Messenger [the Prophet Muḥammed], may God's complete blessings be upon him, the guardian of His revelation and the seal of His messengers, and upon his house and family, did not allow.

In a separate treatise,[2] we have already dealt with the harmony of philosophy and religion, indicating how religion commands the study of

---

1. The Arabic *Shari'a* can also be translated as *Law* or *Holy Law*.
2. That is *Faṣl al-Maqāl*, translated by George F. Hourani as *On the Harmony of Religion and Philosophy* (London: Messrs. Luzac & Co., 1961).

philosophy. We maintained there that religion consists of two parts:
133 external and interpreted, and that the external part is incumbent on the
masses, whereas the interpreted is incumbent on the learned. With respect
to that part, it is the duty of the masses to take it at its face value, without
attempting to interpret it. As for the learned, it is not permissible to
divulge their interpretations to the public, as Ali [Ibn Abi Tālib], God be
pleased with him, said: "Address people in a language that they
understand; do you want God and his Messenger to lie?"

Thus, I decided to inquire in this book into those external dogmas
which religion intended the public to uphold, and to investigate in all this,
to the degree to which my energy and capability permit, the intention of
the lawgiver, God's prayer and peace be upon him. For on this issue,
people in [this] religion have been greatly confused, to the point of
splintering into many erring groups and different sects, each group
believing that it is following the original religion and branding whoever
disagrees with it as either a heretic or an unbeliever (*Kāfir*) whose blood
and property are free for all. All this is a departure from the intent of the
lawgiver, occasioned by their mistaken understanding of the intent of
religion.

The most famous of these sects in our time are four: (1) The sect
called the Ash'arite, which is believed by most people of our day to be the
orthodox; (2) that which is called the Mu'tazilite; (3) the group which is
known as the esoteric [Bāṭini]; and (4) the one called the literalist.

All these sects have entertained diverse beliefs about God and
distorted the apparent meaning of many statements of Scripture with
interpretations applied[3] to such beliefs, claiming that[4] these interpretations constitute the original religion that all people were meant to uphold,
and that whoever deviates from them is either an unbeliever or a heretic.
However, if [all such] beliefs were examined and compared with the
intent of religion, it would appear that most of them are novel statements
and heretical interpretations. Of these beliefs I will refer to those which
have acquired the status of obligatory dogma in the Law without which
the faith [of the Muslim] cannot be complete. In all this I will inquire into

3. Or *Tailored to fit.*
4. In manuscript number 129 (hereafter "A"): *Each one of them believes.*

134 the intent of the lawgiver, God's prayer and peace be upon him, excluding what was considered a fundamental principle in religion and one of its dogma, by unsound interpretation.

I begin by defining what the lawgiver intended the public to believe with respect to God Almighty,[5] and the methods that the Precious Book employs to instill belief in them. So let us start with the argument that leads to the existence of the Maker, since it is the first thing that the responsible believer should know. However, prior to this, we should mention the opinions of those famous sects regarding this matter.

We start with the sect that is called the literalist whose followers claim that the method of knowing the existence of God Almighty is by way of report not by reason. In other words, with respect to the belief in His existence, which men are required to assent to, it is sufficient for them to receive it from the lawgiver and accept it on faith, just as they receive from him the states of the hereafter and other matters in which there is no room for reason. It is apparent from the consideration of this wayward sect that it is incapable of understanding the intent of Scripture regarding the method that it laid down for leading everyone to the knowledge of the existence of God Almighty, and through which He summoned all men to believe in Him. For it is evident from more than one verse in the Book of God Almighty that He calls upon men to believe in the existence of the Originator, glory be to Him, through rational arguments detailed specifically therein, such as the saying of the Almighty: "O people, worship your Lord who has created you as well as those who came before you";[6] and as the other saying of the Almighty: "Is there any doubt about Allah, Maker of the heavens and the earth?"[7] in addition to many other verses in the same vein.

It is not open for someone to say: "If this were the duty incumbent
135 upon whoever believes in God; namely, that no man's faith will be

---

5. Ibn Rushd invariably uses the phrase "*blessed and exalted*". I find it easier for the modern ear to use instead "*God Almighty*".

6. Majid Fakhry (trans.), The Qur'an: *A Modern English Version* (Reading: Garnet Publishing, 1997), 2: 20.

7. Qur'an 14: 10. Arberry translates the verse: "Is there any doubt regarding God, the Originator of the heavens and the earth?" *The Koran Interpreted* (London: Oxford University Press, 1964).

acceptable unless he comes to know these arguments, then the Prophet, God's prayer and peace be upon him, would not have called anyone to Islam without first presenting him with these arguments", for all the Arabs accept the existence of the Glorious Originator. It is for this reason that the Almighty says: "If you ask them: 'Who has created the heavens and the earth?', they will reply, 'Allah'."[8] It should be admitted that it is not impossible that there may be some individuals whose intellect is so sluggish and their acumen so dull that they do not understand anything of the religious arguments which [the Prophet], prayer and peace be on him, has set up for the public. But this is the rarest exception. However, if there are such men, they would be required to believe in God by way of report. This, then, is the way of the literalists regarding the external meaning of religion.

The Ash'arites, however, maintain that believing in the existence of God Almighty is only possible through reason. However, in doing so, they adopted certain methods which are not the religious ones that God has drawn attention to and through which He called upon all men to believe in Him. Their most famous method is based on showing that the world is created in time, while the creation of the world, according to them, is based on the claim that bodies are composed of indivisible parts, that the part which cannot be subdivided is created in time and that bodies are created by its creation. However, the method whereby they showed how the indivisible part, which they call the indivisible substance,[9] is created in time is an abstruse one which many of the well-experienced in the art of logic cannot understand, let alone the public. Moreover, it remains a non-demonstrative method and does not lead to certainty about the existence of the Originator, the Almighty.

If we suppose that the world is created, it follows, as they say, that it must necessarily have a Maker[10] who created it. The existence of this Maker, however, raises a doubt that is not within the power of the art of theology (*Kalam*) to dispel. We can neither say that this Maker is eternal or created. He is not created, because a created being would be in need of a

136

---

8. Qur'an 39: 38.
9. Or *atom*.
10. Or *Producer*, (*Fā'il*).

creator, and this one of another creator, and the matter would go on to infinity, which is absurd. Likewise [we cannot say] that He is eternal, because His action which is related to His products would be eternal, thus rendering the products themselves eternal. The existence of the created must be related to a created action unless [the adherents of this sect] admit that there can be a created action due to an eternal agent, since it is necessary that the product be related to the action of the producer, which they do not admit. It is one of their basic premises that that which is conjoined to the created is created. Moreover, if the agent were sometimes acting and sometimes not, there must exist a cause which makes it more liable to be in one state rather than the other. Then, a similar question can be raised regarding this cause, and the cause of this cause, and the matter would go on to infinity.

What the theologians (Mutakallimun) say in response to the claim that the created action was the product of an eternal will does not help them, nor does it dispel this doubt, because the will is different from the action related to the product. If the product were created, then the action related to its production must be created (irrespective of whether we assume that the will is eternal or created), and precede the action or be simultaneous with it. Whichever is the case, they are forced to allow one of three alternatives with respect to the eternal: either a created will and a created action, or a created action and an eternal will, or an eternal action and an eternal will. Now what is created cannot ensue upon an eternal action without an intermediary, assuming we agree with them that it can ensue upon an eternal will. Moreover, to suppose that the will is identical with the action related to the product is irrational. It is similar to supposing a product without a producer, for the action is something other than the agent, the product and the will, and the will is the pre-condition of the action, rather than the action itself. Furthermore, this eternal will must be related to the non-existence of the created object in an infinite time [since the created was non-existent for an infinite time][11] for it cannot be related to what is willed at the time in which it necessitated its coming-to-be, except after a lapse of an infinite time, and what is infinite does not cease. Thus what is willed cannot

137

11. This phrase is deleted in manuscript "B".

become actual unless an infinite time has elapsed – a patent absurdity. This is exactly the proof that the Mutakallimun employed with respect to the creation of the rotations of the celestial [spheres].

Moreover, there must occur in the will, which precedes what is willed and is related to it at a specific time during which it must exist at the time of producing the willed object, a determination to produce that which did not exist prior to that time. If there were not in the willing agent, at the time of action, a state additional to the state it was in at the time the will necessitated no such action, then the occurrence of that action, at that time, would not be more likely than its non-occurrence. Add to this that there is in this reasoning digression and abstruse doubts that even the skilled adepts of the science of theology (*Kalam*) and philosophy, let alone the public, cannot resolve. Were the public, then, required to attain knowledge through these methods, it would be imposing on them what is beyond their capacities.

In addition the methods that these people employed in their discussion of the creation of the world have combined these two characteristics: namely, that they are not such that it is in the nature of the public to accept them, neither are they demonstrative. Accordingly such methods are suitable neither to the learned nor to the public. Thus we draw attention here to that to some extent by saying that the methods that they have followed are twofold. The first, which is the more famous and upon which most of their followers rely, is based on three premises which serve as first principles from which they hope to deduce the creation of the world. The first [premise] states that substances never exist apart from accidents (i.e., they are never divested of them); the second is that accidents are created; and the third is that what cannot exist apart from accidents is created; by which I mean that what cannot be divested of accidents is created.

As for the first premise, which states that substances do not exist apart from accidents, if they mean by it the independent bodies that can be pointed to, then it is true. But if they mean by substance that part which is indivisible (since this is what they designate by the individual substance), then there is considerable doubt concerning it. The existence of an indivisible substance is not self-evident and there are with respect to it many conflicting opinions that are difficult to reconcile. It is not within the power of the art of *Kalam* to disentangle the truth from them; such a job belongs more appropriately to the art of demonstration, and the adepts of this art are very few. Moreover, the arguments which the Ash'arites use in proving the existence of this [indivisible substance] are mostly rhetorical, for their famous argument in support of it states that it is one of the first points known about the elephant, for example, that we say it is larger than the ant, since it has many more parts than those of the ant. If this is so then the elephant is made up of these parts, and it is not one simple entity. Hence when the body is destroyed, it dissolves into them, and when it is constructed, it is constructed out of them.

They committed this error due to the similarity between discontinuous and continuous quantity. They thought that what applies to the former must apply to the latter. However, this is true of numbers only. We say that a number is greater than another by virtue of the many parts or units it has. But with regard to the continuous quantity this is not true. For this reason, we say of the continuous quantity that it is larger and bigger, but not that it is more or less, whereas in the case of numbers, we say that they are more or less, but not larger or smaller. On this view all things would be numbers and there would be no continuous magnitude to begin with; in which case geometry would be the same as arithmetic. It is self-evident, however, that each magnitude is divisible into two halves; by which I mean the three magnitudes which are the line, the plane, and the body [or solid]. Furthermore, it is the continuous magnitude that may
139 have in its middle an end where both extremities of the two parts meet; and this is not possible in the case of numbers.

However, we find this position contradicted by the fact that the body and all the parts of the continuous magnitude are susceptible of division; and whatever is divisible is divisible either into something divisible or something indivisible. If it is divisible into something indivisible, then we have found the part which cannot be divided any further; but if it is divided into something which is divisible, then the question recurs with respect to this divisible: "Is it divisible into something divisible or something indivisible?" If it is divisible *ad infinitum*, then there would be infinite parts in the finite thing. But it is elementary knowledge that the parts of what is finite are also finite.

One of the abstruse questions which must be addressed to them is this: "If the part which is indivisible were created, then what is the bearer of this creation (*Ḥudūth*)?" Creation is an accident among other accidents, and once the created object exists, creation ceases. For it is one of their principles that accidents do not exist apart from substances; therefore they are forced to concede that creation is from some existing entity and out of an existing entity.

They might also be asked, "If an existing thing can exist apart from not-being, then to what does the action of the agent attach?" for there is no intermediary between being and not-being, according to them. If this is the case, and the action of the agent does not attach, according to them, to not-being, nor to what already exists in reality, it must attach to an entity intermediate between being and not-being. This is what forced the Mu'tazilites to claim that there is in not-being an entity of some sort. They[12] are also forced to admit the existence in actuality of that which does not exist in actuality. In fact both sects[13] are forced to admit the existence of the void.

These problems, as you see, cannot be resolved by the art of dialectic. 140 Therefore this [view] must not be laid down as a principle for the knowledge of God Almighty, especially with reference to the public, for the method of knowing God Almighty, as we shall show shortly, is much clearer than this one.

* * *

The second premise, which states that all accidents are created, is open to doubt; the obscurity of this claim is similar to that of bodies, for we have only seen some bodies created as we have accidents; there is no difference, between the two in passing[14] from the seen to the unseen.[15] Thus, if it is necessary in the case of accidents to apply our judgment of what is seen to what is unseen (i.e., to make a judgment about the creation of what we do

---

12. Ibn Rushd here resumes his discussion of the Ash'arites' position.
13. The Mu'tazilites and the Ash'arites.
14. Ibn Rushd uses *al-Nuqla* to denote an inductive inference from the seen to the unseen.
15. Ibn Rushd uses the term "the seen" to refer to what falls within the scope of our sense-experience and the term "the unseen" to refer to what does not fall within that scope. Sometimes he uses "the seen" to refer to this world and "the unseen" to refer to the intelligible world.

not see by analogy with what we see), then we should be able to do so with respect to bodies, dispensing altogether with inferring from the creation of accidents the creation of bodies. For with regard to the heavenly body, whose analogy to the seen is itself subject to doubt, the doubt surrounding its accidents is similar to the doubt surrounding its creation itself, since neither its creation nor that of its accidents has been perceived. Therefore, we must investigate this matter by reference to its motion; and this is the method that leads those who seek the knowledge of God Almighty with certainty. Indeed, it is the method of the select and the one for which God has favored Abraham, peace be upon him, in His saying: "Thus We show Abraham the Kingdom of the heavens and the earth, that he might be of those possessed of certainty,"[16] since all the doubt has revolved around the heavenly bodies, and most of the theoreticians who studied them concluded that they are gods.

Moreover, time is one of the accidents although it is difficult to imagine its creation, because every being must be preceded by not-being in time. Accordingly, if the not-being of an entity precedes the thing itself, it cannot be imagined except with reference to time. Furthermore it is difficult to imagine the place the world occupies as created (assuming that every occupant must precede the place it occupies), for if the void exists, as maintained by those who believe that the void is identical with place, 141 then its creation must be preceded by another void, if it is supposed to be created. And if the place is taken to be the boundary of the body surrounding what is in place, as the holders of the second view maintain,[17] then it is necessary that this body should exist in place, and that this body would then be in need of another body, and the matter will go on to infinity.

All these are abstruse doubts. However, the arguments whereby [the Ash'arites] seek to refute the claim that the accidents are eternal are convincing for those who maintain the eternity of what is perceived as created; by which I mean those who claim that all accidents are not created. For they say: "If the accidents that appear to the senses as created were not created, then they would have to be either in transition from one

16. Qur'an 6: 75.
17. That is, Aristotle and his followers. See *Physics IV*, 217a–5.

place to another, or latent in the place where they appeared before appearing." Then they proceed to refute these two alternatives, thinking that they have demonstrated that all accidents are created. However, what simply follows from their statement is that those accidents which appear to be created are created, but not those that do not appear to be created, or those of which the creation of their accidents is in doubt, as in the case of the accidents pertaining to the heavenly bodies, such as their motions, their forms and so on. Thus, their arguments for the creation of all the accidents are reducible to the analogy between the seen and the unseen, (which is a rhetorical argument); except where the inference is reasonable in itself, and that is possible only after ascertaining the equivalence[18] of the natures of both the seen and the unseen.

* * *

The third premise, which states that that which cannot exist without accidents must be created, is an ambiguous one, because it can be understood in two ways. The first meaning refers to that which cannot exist without the genus of accidents, though it might exist without a particular singular accident; the second refers to what does not exist without a specific accident *pointed to* directly, as when you say: "That which does not exist without this blackness I am *pointing to*". This second meaning is sound; 142 whatever cannot exist without an accident that one can point to and is created, its subject must necessarily be created too, for, if [the subject] were eternal, it would be devoid of that accident, but we have assumed it not to exist without it. This is an impossible absurdity. However, from the first interpretation, which they favor, it does not follow that the substratum is created; namely, that which is not free of the genus of accidents. For it is possible to imagine the same substratum, that is, the body, occupied successively by accidents which are infinite, whether opposed to each other or not. This is like speaking of infinite motions, as many of the ancients used to believe the universe is formed, one [world] after another.[19] For this reason, when the later Mutakallimun realized that this premise is tenuous,

---

18. *Istiwā* in this connection implies that the nature of the seen and that of the unseen are equivalent and the laws that apply to the one apply to the other.
19. As held by some Presocratics, such as Heraclitus and Empedocles.

they proceeded to tighten and strengthen it by showing that, as they contended, it is not possible for an infinite number of accidents to exist successively in one substratum. They claimed that there could not exist in that substratum, on this assumption, an accident to which one can point without this accident being preceded by an infinite number of accidents, which would lead to the impossibility of the existence of that which actually exists (namely that which one can point to), for it could not exist except after what is infinite has come to an end. However, since that which is infinite does not come to an end, it follows that that which is pointed to does not exist; I mean, that which is supposed to exist. For example, were the present motion of the heavenly body preceded by an infinite number of motions, the present motion of the heavenly body could not have happened. They have illustrated that by the case of one man saying to another: "I do not give you this *dinar* [20] until I have given you an infinite number of *dinars* before it." Thus it is not possible ever for that man to give him that *dinar* which is pointed to. However, this illustration is incorrect because it involves positing a beginning and an end, while positing what is between them as infinite. The utterance of that [man] actually took place in a 143 definite time, and his giving him the *dinar* took place in a definite time too. Therefore he laid as a condition that he will give him the *dinar* at a time between which and the time of his utterance, infinite periods of time had intervened, during which he is supposed to have given him an infinite number of *dinars*, which is absurd. The example shows that there is no analogy between it and the point it is supposed to illustrate.

As for their claim that that which comes to be after the coming to be of an infinite number of things cannot possibly exist; it is not true in all cases. For things in which some parts precede others are said to exist in two ways: either cyclically or rectilinearly. Those that take place in a cyclical fashion must be supposed to be infinite, unless they are impeded by some thing. For example, if there is a sunrise, there has been a sunset, and if there is a sunset, there has been a sunrise; and if there is a sunrise, there has been a sunrise. Similarly if there is a cloud, there was vapor rising from the ground; and if there is vapor rising from the ground, the ground

20. An ancient Roman silver coin, or *denarius*.

was wet; and if the ground was wet, then there was rain; and if there was rain, there was a cloud; and if there was a cloud, then there was a cloud. As for what takes place in a rectilinear fashion, as when one human being begets another human being who in turn begets another human being; if that takes place essentially, then it is not true that the matter could go on to infinity. For if the first of the causes did not exist, the last could not exist either. However, if the existence [of the first] was accidental, as when the human being comes to be in reality from an agent other than his father, who is his originator – the role of the father being the role of the instrument with respect to the artisan[21] – then it is not impossible, were that agent to act infinitely, for an infinite number of people to be produced by means of a variety of instruments. However, this is not the place to discuss all this. We mention it merely to show that, what those people imagined to be a proof, is not really one. It is not even one of the
144 arguments that are suitable for the public; by which I mean the simple demonstrations whereby God has required all His worshipers to believe in Him. Thus it will have become evident to you from this that this method is not technically demonstrable or religious.

* * *

The second method was introduced by Abu al-Ma'ālī[22] in his treatise known as *al-Niẓāmiah*. It is based on two premises. The first states that it is possible for the world, with everything in it, to be the opposite of what it actually is [for example, it is possible for it to be smaller or bigger than it is now],[23] or in a shape other than its present one, or to contain a number of bodies other than the actual one, or to be such that every movable object moves in the opposite direction to its present motion. It would, then, be possible, [for example] for a stone to move upwards, and for fire to move downwards, and for the eastern movement to be western, and the western to be eastern. The second premise states that what is possible is created, and has a creator; by which I mean, an agent who made it more the susceptible of one of the two possibilities, rather than the other.

21. Or *agent*.
22. That is Al-Juwayni (d.1086), Ash'arite teacher of Al-Ghazāli.
23. This part is missing in manuscript number 133 (hereafter "B").

As for the first premise, it is rhetorical and appears so at first sight. With respect to some parts of the world, the falsity of this premise is self-evident, as, for instance, in supposing man to exist in a different form than his present one. With respect to other parts, the matter is doubtful, such as [supposing] the eastern movement being western and the western being eastern, since this is not self-evident. It might have had a cause which is unknowable in itself, or it might be one of the causes which are hidden 145 from man's purview. It seems that what initially appears to the person who investigates these matters is similar to what appears to those who study the parts of manufactured objects without having the skills of their manufacturers. Such people have a preconceived notion that the constituents of these manufactured objects, or most of them, could be otherwise, [yet they continue] to generate the same actions for which they were manufactured; I mean, their purpose. If it were so, there would be no wisdom in what is manufactured. The manufacturer and those who share with him some knowledge of the science [of producing these things], would of course think that the matter is otherwise, and that there is nothing in what is manufactured save what is necessary; or if not necessary, that it exists so that the manufactured object may be more complete or better. Indeed this is the meaning of art. It seems that the creatures resemble what is manufactured in this sense. May the Great Creator be glorified!

In so far as this premise is rhetorical, there may be no harm in using it to convince all people; but in so far as it is false and nullifies the wisdom of the Artisan, it is not appropriate for them. It abolishes wisdom, because wisdom is nothing more than the knowledge of the causes of existing things, and if there are no necessary causes which necessitate the existence of these things, in the form in which those of their kind exist, then there is no knowledge here that distinguishes the Wise Creator from any other. Besides, if there are no necessary causes entering into the constitution of manufactured objects, there would be no crafts to begin with, nor would wisdom be attributed to the artisan rather than to the one who is not an artisan. Indeed, what wisdom would there be in man, if all his actions and deeds were to result from whichever organ happens to be, or even came to be without an organ, so that seeing could take place, for example, through the ear just as easily as through the eye, and the smell through the eye exactly as it is through the nose? All this nullifies wisdom as well as the reason for which the Almighty called Himself Wise, may He be Exalted and His names be hallowed.

* * *

146 It might be observed that Ibn Sina accepts this premise in a certain respect, since he believes that every existing entity, other than the Agent, if considered in itself, is possible and contingent. The contingent is of two types: one is contingent by virtue of its agent, and the other is necessary by virtue of its agent, though possible in itself, while what is necessary in every respect is the First Agent. However, this claim is patently absurd because what is possible in itself and its essence, cannot become necessary by virtue of its agent, unless the nature of what is possible becomes that of the necessary. If it is said that he means by saying "possible in itself" that which, when its agent is imagined to be removed, it is itself removed,[24] we would assert that this removal is impossible. This, however, is not the place to argue with this man; what led us to argue with him concerning the things he has invented forced us to mention him. Let us return to the matter at hand, then.

As for the second premise, which states that what is contingent[25] is created, this too is not self-evident. Indeed, the philosophers disagreed about it, Plato allowing a contingent thing to exist eternally, while Aristotle did not allow it. This is a very abstruse question. Its truth does not become evident except to the people of the art of demonstration, who are the scholars (*al-'Ūlamā*)[26] whom God [Almighty][27] has favored with His knowledge and supported their testimony with His own testimony and that of His angels in the Precious Book.

As for Abū al-Ma'āli, he sought to explain this premise by recourse to other premises, one of which is that the contingent must have a determinant (*Mukhassis*[28]) to make it the likely recipient of one rather

24. That is, it becomes non-existent.
25. Or *possible.*
26. Or *scientists.*
27. Deleted in "A" and "B".
28. *Mukhassis,* someone to determine or specify it.

than the other of two contingent attributes. The second [premise] is that
147 this determinant cannot be but a willing agent; and the third [premise] is
that what exists as a result of will is created. He [Abū al-Maʿāli] then
explained how the contingent derives from the will, that is, from a willing
agent, by virtue of the fact that every action is either from nature or from
will. However, nature does not cause one of two similar possibilities
(meaning that it brings about one to the exclusion of its like), but rather
both. For example, scammony[29] does not purge the bile that is on the right
side of the body rather than that which is on the left side; whereas the will
determines one thing rather than its like. [Abū al-Maʿāli,] then, added that
the world is the same whether it is in the place where it is now, within the
milieu in which it was created (meaning the void), or is in another place
within that void. From this he inferred that the world is created by will.

The premise stating that the will is what determines the one rather
than the other of two comparable instances is correct, but the one stating
that the world is surrounded by a void is false; or at least, not self-evident.
Moreover, [Abū al-Maʿāli's] positing of the void leads to a repugnant
result, according to them; namely that the void is eternal, since if it was
created it would require another void.

However, the premise stating that nothing issues from the will except a
created object is not obvious, for the actual will exists along with the action
which produces the willed object itself, since will is a relative concept. It has
been shown that if one of two correlatives existed in actuality, the other
would exist in actuality as well, such as the father and the son; but if one of
them existed potentially, the other would have to exist in potentiality also.
Should the will, which is in actuality, be created, then the willed object
must necessarily be created [in actuality].[30] Furthermore, should the will,
which is in actuality, be eternal, then the willed, which is in actuality, will
be eternal. With regard to the will which precedes what is willed, it is a will
in potentiality; by which I mean a will whose object has not come into being
actually, since this will has not been conjoined to the action which
148 necessitates the emergence of the willed object. It is clear, then, that if its

---

29. *Convolvulus Scammonia* which is a twining plant whose dried sap is used for the purging of the
bile.
30. Deleted in "B".

willed object came into being, the will is in a state different from what it was in before its willed object came into being actually, since it is the cause of the creation of the willed object through the mediation of the action. Thus, should the Mutakallimun posit that the will is created, it follows necessarily that the willed object is created also.

It seems that the Scripture (*al-Sharʿ*) does not go that far in explaining those things to the public. For this reason it does not refer explicitly to either an eternal or a created will; rather, it refers to what is more obvious; namely, that the will [brings forth existing beings][31] which are created, as in the saying of the Almighty: "Indeed, when We want a thing to be, We just say to it: "Be", and it comes to be."[32] That this is the case is due to the fact that the common people do not understand the meaning of existing things created by an eternal will; indeed, the truth is that Scripture has not stated explicitly whether the will is created or is eternal, since this is one of the ambiguous issues for the majority of people.[33] The Mutakallimun do not have a single conclusive proof to show the impossibility of the subsistence of a created will in an eternal being, because the principle to which they appeal in denying the subsistence of a created will in an eternal being is the premise whose weakness we have already exposed; namely, that that which cannot exist without created accidents is created. We will explain this point more fully in our discussion of the will.

From all this, it will have become evident to you, then, that the Ashʿarites' famous methods, purporting to lead to the knowledge of God Almighty, are not theoretically certain [nor are they religiously certain].[34] This is obvious to whoever investigates the types of arguments to which the Precious Book draws attention regarding this matter (that is, the knowledge of the existence of the Artisan), by which I mean that, when the religious methods are investigated carefully, they are found to include, at most, two characteristics: certainty and simplicity rather than complexity, I mean, having few premises, whereby their conclusions are close to their first premises.

31. Deleted in "S".
32. Qur'an 16: 40.
33. The reference is to the Qur'an 3: 5, which distinguishes between ambiguous (*Mutashābihāt*) and unambiguous (*Muḥkamāt*) verses.
34. Deleted in "B".

* * *

149 As regards the Sufis, their methods of investigation are not theoretical, composed of premises and syllogisms. Rather, they claim that the knowledge of God, as well as other entities, is something cast in the soul once it has been cleansed of its worldly appetites and upon focusing its attention on the desired object. In support of this view, they appeal to the external meaning of many religious texts, like the saying of the Almighty: "And fear Allah and He will teach you,"[35] and: "And those who strive in Our cause We shall guide in Our ways,"[36] and: "O you who believe, if you fear Allah, He will provide you with a criterion"[37] [to distinguish right from wrong], and many other texts like these believed to buttress this point.

However, we hold that, even if we admit the existence of this method, it is not common to all men, *qua* men. Indeed if they were intended to follow this method, the method of theoretical investigation would have been dispensed with altogether and its existence in the minds of men would have been in vain. Yet the Qur'an in its entirety is but a call to theoretical investigation and consideration and an admonition to resort to these theoretical methods. It is true, we do not deny that the mortification of the flesh might be a precondition of sound theoretical investigations, just as health might be, but the suppression of appetites is not what yields knowledge in itself, although it is still a precondition of it, just as health is a precondition of learning but is not what yields it. It is from this perspective that Scripture has called for this method and strongly urged its adoption in its entirety, (meaning in matters of action, not that it is sufficient in itself, as these people have imagined). If it is useful in theoretical matters, it will be in the manner we have just mentioned. And this is obvious to whoever is fair and considers the matter in itself.

* * *

With respect to the Mu'tazilites, none of their books have reached us in this island to be able to investigate the methods they followed in this

35. Qur'an 2: 282.
36. Qur'an 29: 69.
37. Qur'an 8: 29.

matter. It is likely that their methods are of the same type as those of the Ash'arites.

150 If it be asked, now that it has become evident that none of these methods is the religious method, through which religion has called upon all mankind, despite the differences in their natures, to confess the existence of the Almighty Creator, "What, then, is the religious method which the Precious Book has recommended and which was adopted by the Companions of the Prophet, may God be pleased with them?"

We would answer that the method[38] which the Precious Book recommends and calls all mankind to follow is found, if the Precious Book is reviewed, to consist of two kinds. The first is the method of providing for man, and creating all existing things for his sake. Let us call it the argument from providence. The second method [refers to] the manifest invention of the substances of existing beings, such as the invention of life in inanimate matter, as well as sense-perception and intellect. Let us call this the argument from invention.

The first method is founded on two principles; one of them is that all existing beings, which are found here below, are suited to man's existence, and the second principle is that this suitability is necessarily due to an Agent both intending and willing, since it is not possible for this suitability to be due to fortuitous chance. As for its being suited to man's existence, one becomes certain of it from the consideration of the suitability of night and day and the sun and the moon to man's existence. Add to that the suitability of the four seasons to him, and the place in which he exists, namely the earth. Moreover, it is evident that this suitability exists with respect to many animals, plants, inanimate objects and many particulars like the rain, the rivers and the seas; and, in short, the earth, water, fire, and air. Moreover, providence is evident in the human and animal organs,

151 I mean, their being suited to his life and existence. On the whole, then, the knowledge of the utility of existing things falls within this category. That is why it is incumbent on those who want to acquire a complete knowledge of God Almighty to inquire into the usefulness of all existing things.

38. In "A": *the methods.*

With respect to the argument from invention, it includes [the investigation of] the existence of the animal kind as a whole, and that of the plants and the heavens. This method is based on two principles existing potentially in human nature.

The first is that all these existing entities are invented, which, in the case of animals and plants, is self-evident, as the Almighty says: "Surely, those whom you call upon, besides Allah, will never create a fly, even if they band together. [And if a fly should rob them of something, they cannot retrieve it from it. How weak is the invoker and the invoked!]".[39] We see inanimate objects in which life then appears and so we know for certain that there is here a Producer of life and a Gracious Giver of it, who is God Almighty. As for the heavens, we know from their ceaseless motions that they are commanded to attend to whatever exists here below and to be subservient to us. Furthermore, the subservient and the commanded are necessarily invented by someone else.

The second principle is that for everything invented there is an inventor.

From these two principles it correctly follows that for every existing entity there is an agent who is its inventor. Evidence for this conclusion is found in the sheer number of invented entities. That is why it is incumbent on those who seek a true knowledge of God to know the essences of things, in order to understand the true meaning of invention in all existing entities. For whoever does not know the truth about the thing, does not know the real meaning of invention. To this the reference in the saying of the Almighty refers: "Have they not considered the kingdom of the heavens and the earth and all the things Allah has created, [and how perhaps their appointed term may have drawn near]?"[40] Moreover, whoever pursues carefully[41] the meaning of wisdom in the existence of every individual entity – by which I mean that the knowledge of the cause for the sake of which that existing entity was created and the final purpose intended for it – will have a more complete knowledge of the argument from providence.

39. Qur'an 22: 73.
40. Qur'an 7: 184.
41. In "S": *follows.*

152   These two arguments, then, are the arguments favored by religion. That the verses in which the Precious Book draws attention to the arguments leading to the existence of the Almighty Artisan are confined to these two kinds is evident to whoever studies the verses given in the Precious Book in this regard. Were these verses to be examined, they would be found to be of three types: (1) either verses referring to the argument from providence, or (2) verses referring to the argument from invention, or (3) verses combining both types of reasoning.

Of the verses that refer only to the argument from providence is the saying of the Almighty:

> Have We not made the earth as a couch for you?
> And the mountains as pegs?
> [And created you in pairs?
> And made your sleep a period of rest?
> And made the night as a garment?
> And made the day a source of livelihood?
> And built above you seven mighty [heavens]?
> And created a shining lamp?
> And brought down from the rain-clouds abundant water?
> To bring forth thereby grain and vegetation?]
> And luxuriant gardens?[42]

Or His saying: "Blessed is He who placed in the heaven constellations and placed in it a lamp and an illuminating moon."[43] And the saying of the Almighty:

> Let Man consider his nourishment.
> [We poured the water abundantly;
> Then, We split the earth wide open;
> Then caused the grain to grow therein;
> Together with vines green vegetation;
> And olives and palm trees;
> And gardens with dense trees,
> And fruits and grass,
> For your enjoyment and that of your cattle.]"[44]

42. Qur'an 78: 6–16. The verses in brackets are not cited, but are understood.
43. Qur'an 25: 61.
44. Qur'an 80: 24–33. See note 42 above.

The Qur'an is replete with similar verses.

As for the verses which refer only to the argument from invention, they include the saying of the Almighty: "So let man consider of what he was created. He was created from flowing water;"[45] and His saying: "Will they, then, not consider the camels, how they were created?"[46] or like His saying: "O people, an example has been given; so listen to it. Surely, those whom you call upon, besides Allah, will never create a fly, even if they band together."[47] In this vein also is the saying of the Almighty reporting the words of Abraham: "I turn my face towards Him who fashioned the heavens and the earth",[48] to which may be added innumerable verses.

Those verses which combine both references are also numerous, in fact they are the majority, like the saying of the Almighty: "O people, worship your Lord who has created you as well as those who came before you [so that you may guard against evil; Who has made the earth a couch for you, and the heavens a canopy, and Who sent down water from the sky, bringing forth by it a variety of fruits as a provision for you.] Therefore do not knowingly set up equals to Allah."[49] His saying "Who has created you as well as those who came before you" is a pointer to the argument of invention, and His saying "Who has made the earth a couch for you, and the heavens a canopy"[50] is a pointer to the argument from providence. This is also true of the saying of the Almighty: "A sign unto them is the dead land, that We revived and brought out of it grain, from which they eat"[51] and His saying: "Those who [remember Allah standing, sitting or lying on their sides,][52] reflecting upon the creation of the heavens and the earth [saying]: 'Our Lord you did not create this in vain. Glory be to You! Save us from the torment of the Fire.'"[53] Most of the verses that bear this connotation contain both types of evidence.

153

---

45. Qur'an 86: 5.
46. Qur'an 88: 17. [And heaven, how it was raised up? And the mountains, how they were hoisted? And the earth, how it was leveled?]
47. Qur'an 22: 73.
48. Qur'an 6: 79.
49. Qur'an 2: 20–23.
50. *Ibid.*
51. Qur'an 36: 33.
52. Deleted in all manuscripts.
53. Qur'an 3: 191.

Thus, this method is the straight path by which God has called upon men to know His existence and has alerted them to it by what He implanted in their primitive natures of [capacities to] understand this meaning. The reference to this original primitive nature implanted in the natures of men is contained in the saying of the Almighty: "And [remember] when your Lord brought forth from the loins of the children of Adam their posterity [and made them testify against themselves. He said: 'Am I not your Lord?' They said: 'Yes, we testify.']"[54] That is why it might be required from whoever wants to obey God by believing in Him and listening to what His Messengers have brought forward to adopt this method, so as to become one of the learned scholars who testify to God's lordship, along with His own testimony and that of His angels, as the Almighty says: "Allah bears witness that there is no god but He, and so do the angels and men of learning. He upholds justice. There is no god but He, the Mighty and Wise One."[55] Evidence that existing entities point to Him in these two respects is the praise indicated in the saying of the Almighty: "And there is nothing which does not celebrate His praise; but you do not understand their praise."[56]

It has become clear from these arguments that the evidence for the existence of the Artisan is confined to these two types; namely, the argument from providence and the argument from invention. It has also become clear that these two methods correspond exactly to the method used by the select (meaning the learned), and that of the general public. Where the two types of knowledge differ is in the details; the general public are content, as far as knowing providence and invention is concerned, with what is known through primary knowledge, which is derived from sense-impressions. The learned, however, add to what is known of existing things through sense-perception that which is known through demonstration by reference to providence and invention. Some scholars have gone so far as to claim that the knowledge of the organs of human beings and animals they have achieved is close to thousands and thousands of times in utility. And if this is the case, then this method is the

54. Qur'an 7: 172.
55. Qur'an 3: 18.
56. Qur'an 17: 44.

religious and natural one, and the one that was brought forth by the Messengers and proclaimed by the sacred Scriptures. Not only are the learned superior to the general public when it comes to those two demonstrations in point of number, but also in point of the depth of their knowledge of specific objects. The general public theorize about the existing entities in the same manner as they theorize about the manufactured objects; about the art of making them they have no knowledge. All they know is that they are manufactured and that they have an existing maker. By contrast the learned are those who theorize about the manufactured objects on the basis of their knowledge of how such objects are made and the wisdom behind making them. There is no doubt that whoever possesses this kind of knowledge of manufactured objects knows the Artisan, *qua* Artisan, better than those who merely know that these objects are manufactured. As for the materialists,[57] those who deny the existence of the Almighty Artisan, their case is similar to those who merely sensed the existence of certain manufactured objects, but did not admit that they were manufactured. Instead they attributed what they saw in them of workmanship to chance and to whatever was the product of spontaneity.

---

57. *Al-Dahriyah.* In the Arabic sources, this term refers to an undetermined group of naturalists and materialists who denied the existence of God and believed in chance.

2

On God's unity

155 Should someone ask: "If this is the religious method for knowing the existence of the Creator, may He be glorified, what then is the religious method [for knowing] His oneness too, which is the knowledge that there is no god but He? For, this negation is a notion additional to the positive one implicit in this word, and this positive meaning has been demonstrated in the preceding discourse. Now what is intended by affirming the negation?" Our answer is that, as for denying the divinity to anyone other than He, the religious method in this regard is the one that God Almighty has spoken of in His Precious Book in three verses. The first is the saying of the Almighty: "Were there in them both [heaven and earth] other gods than Allah, they would surely have been ruined."[1] The second is the saying of the Almighty: "Allah did not take to Himself a child and there was never another god with Him; or else each god would have carried off what he has created, and some of them would have risen against the others. Exalted be Allah above what they describe!"[2] The third is the saying of the Almighty: "Say: 'If there were other gods with Him, as they say, then surely they would have sought access to the Lord of the Throne.'"[3]

1. Qur'an 21: 22.
2. Qur'an 23: 91.
3. Qur'an 17: 42.

The meaning of the first verse is implanted in the instincts [of man] by nature. It is self-evident that if there are two kings, the actions of each one being the same as those of the other, it would not be possible [for them] to manage the same city, for there cannot result from two agents of the same kind[4] one and the same action. It follows necessarily that if they acted together, the city would be ruined,[5] unless one of them acted while the other remained inactive; and this is incompatible with the attribute of

156 divinity. When two actions of the same kind converge on one substratum, that substratum is corrupted necessarily. [This] is the meaning of the saying of the Almighty: "Were there in them both [heaven and earth] other gods than Allah, they would surely have been ruined."[6]

As for His saying: "Or else each god would have carried off what he has created",[7] it is His answer to whoever posits many gods performing differing actions. For that would necessitate that no single entity will result from gods performing differing actions, and are not obedient to each other. And since the world is one single entity, it could not have resulted from gods with diverse actions.

As for the saying of the Almighty "Say: 'If there were other gods with Him, as they say, then surely they would have sought access to the Lord of the Throne'",[8] it is similar to the first verse in that it is also a proof of the impossibility of the existence of two gods whose actions are one and the same. The meaning of this verse is that were there [in heaven and earth] gods other than the existing God, capable of bringing forth the world and creating it, such that their relationship to this world is the same as that of the Creator to it, then they would have to be on the Throne with Him. Thus there would have been two similar beings having the same relationship to the same locus.[9] Two similar things cannot be related to the same place in the same way, for if the relationship is identical, the *relata* are identical. [The *relata*] cannot have an identical relation to the same locus, just as they cannot occupy the same locus (should they be of

4. Or *from two similar agents.*
5. Or *fall apart.*
6. Qur'an 21: 22.
7. Qur'an 23: 91.
8. Qur'an 17: 42.
9. That is, the Throne.

the kind that occupies a locus), although the relationship of God to the Throne is the opposite of this type of relation; by which I mean that the Throne subsists in Him, not that He subsists in the Throne. For this reason, God Almighty says: "His throne encompasses the heavens and the earth, and their preservation does not burden Him."[10] This, then, is the argument that is ingrained by instinct and religion with respect to the knowledge of the oneness of God. The difference between the learned and the ordinary people, with respect to this argument, is that the learned

157 know about the origination of the world and the existence of some of its parts for the sake of other parts, whereby they resemble a single body, more than the ordinary public knows about them. It is to this meaning that the Almighty refers at the end of the verse: "Glory be to Him and may He be greatly exalted above what they say. The seven heavens, the earth and what is in them praise Him, and there is nothing which does not celebrate His praise; but you do not understand their praise. He is indeed Clement, All-forgiving."[11]

As for the argument that the Ash'arites infer from this verse by contrivance and call the argument of exclusion, it does not function the way natural and religious arguments do. It does not function naturally, because what they say in this regard does not constitute a proof. Moreover, it does not function the way religious arguments do, because the masses cannot understand what they[12] mean by it, let alone be convinced by it. For, they say: "If there were two [gods] or more, it would be possible for them to disagree, and if they disagree, their [disagreement] would involve only three alternatives: (1) either they would all accomplish what they desired, or (2) no one would attain what he desires, or (3) only one of them would accomplish what he desires but not the other." They add that it is impossible that none of them could accomplish what he desires, for if this were the case then the world would neither be existing nor not-existing. Moreover, it is impossible for what they both want to come to be, for the world would then be existing and not-existing at the same time. Thus, the only alternative left is that what one of them

10. Qur'an 2: 255.
11. Qur'an 17: 43.
12. The Ash'arites.

desires will be accomplished, while what the other desires will be thwarted. Accordingly, the one whose will is not fulfilled is impotent, and the impotent cannot be a god.

The weakness of this argument consists in that, just as it is possible, in principle, for the [two gods] to disagree, by analogy with visible agents, it is also possible for them to agree, which is more appropriate for the gods than to disagree. Now, if they agree on making the world, they would be like two artisans who agree on manufacturing one artifact; and if this is the case, then it must be said that their actions, when they are both in agreement, are concurrent, since they converge on one object. However, one might say: "Perhaps one of them makes part of the [artifact] while the other makes some other [part]; or perhaps they take turns." But this objection is not suited to the general public. The answer in this case to those dialecticians who doubt that intent,[13] is to say: "The one who is capable of creating[14] the part is also capable of creating the whole. In the final analysis, the matter is reducible to the capacity of [the two gods] to do everything. Either they agree or they disagree, irrespective of the manner of their cooperation in action. As for acting by taking turns, it is a deficiency in the status of each one of them. It is more likely that if they were two [gods], there would also be two worlds. Now the world is one, hence the Agent is one, for one single action can only come from one [agent]. Thus, it should not be understood from the saying of the Almighty "And some of them would have risen against the others,"[15] that it applies only to differences in actions, but also to their agreement in actions. For harmonious actions combine together to achieve one goal, exactly as conflicting actions do. This is the difference between how we understand this verse and how the Mutakallimun understand it, even though one might find in Abū al-Maʿālī's words a reference to what we have stated.[16]

Moreover, what might show you that the argument which the Mutakallimun derived from the above verse is not the one implied in the

---

13. The Mutakallimun.
14. Literally, *inventing.*
15. Qurʾan 23: 91.
16. Abu al-Maʿālī, also known as Al-Juwayni (d.1086) is the leading Ashʿarite and author of the *Nizamiyah Treatise*, mentioned later on in *al-Kashf.*

verse, is that the absurdity to which [their argument leads is different from that absurdity to which][17] the argument mentioned in that verse leads. For the absurdity which they allege to be implicit in the verse's argument, is more than one single absurdity, since they divide the matter into three different parts, whereas there is no such division in that verse. The argument that they[18] use in this regard is the one called by the logicians the conditional, disjunctive syllogism, while they call it in their art the argument of measuring and division. The argument that the verse implies is the one known in the art of logic as conditional conjunctive syllogism, which is different from the disjunctive one. Whoever knows anything about this art will see the difference between the two arguments.

159   Moreover, the absurdities to which their argument leads are different from the absurdity to which the argument of the Book leads, because the absurdity to which their argument leads is that the world is neither existing [nor not-existing, or is existing][19] and not-existing, or that God is powerless and vanquished. These are invariable impossibilities due to the absurdity of more than one [god], while the impossibility that the argument of the Book leads to is not an invariable impossibility, but rather an impossibility contingent upon a specific time; namely, that the world should be inexistent *at the time of existence.* It is as though had the Almighty said: "Were there in them [heaven and earth] other gods than Allah",[20] then the world would have been inexistent now, but He excluded that it is not inexistent.[21] It follows that there is no God but one.

This discussion has exhibited the various methods by means of which the Scripture has called upon people to confess the existence of the glorious Creator, and to deny the divinity of any one other than He. These are the two meanings implied in the profession of divine unity,[22] [There is no god but Allah, and whoever utters this word][23] and assents to

---

17. Deleted in "B".
18. Meaning the Ash'arites, or the Mutakallimun generally.
19. Deleted in "A".
20. Qur'an 21: 22.
21. That is, He excluded or made an exception of the non-existence of the world, since it already exists.
22. *Al-Tawḥīd.*
23. Deleted in "A".

the two meanings implicit in it in the manner we have just described is a true Muslim, whose creed is the Muslim creed. But he whose creed is not based on these arguments, even if he assents to this profession, is, compared to a true Muslim, a Muslim equivocally.

3

On [God's] attributes

As for the attributes which the Precious Book has proclaimed in describing the Artisan, the Originator of the world, they are the attributes of perfection used in describing human beings, and these are seven: knowledge, life, power, will, hearing, vision, and speech.

As for knowledge, the Precious Book has drawn attention to the manner of referring to it in the saying of the Almighty: "Does He not know what He has created, though He is the All-Subtle, the All-Informed?"[1] This manner of reference stems from the way the parts of the manufactured object are organized; namely that they are made for each other's sake, and in so far as they are all conducive to the intended usefulness of that manufactured [object], point to the fact that they were not produced by nature, but rather by an Artisan who arranged all that precedes the end in advance of the end.[2] Hence it is necessary that He should know it. For instance, when a person looks at a house and sees that its foundation was made for the sake of the walls, and the walls for the sake of the ceiling, he will know that the house was made by an expert in the art of masonry.

This attribute [of knowledge] is an eternal attribute, since it is not permissible that the Glorious One be characterized by it for a given

---

1. Qur'an 67: 14.
2. Or *purpose.*

period of time only. But one must not delve deeply into this matter and repeat what the Mutakallimun have said to the effect that He knows the created at the time of its creation by means of an eternal knowledge. For it would follow from this [claim] that [His] knowledge of the created [world], at the time of its not-being and the time of its being, is one and the same knowledge. But this is absurd because knowledge is necessarily consequent upon existence. Accordingly, since what exists sometimes exists in actuality and sometimes in potentiality, it follows that knowledge 161 of the two modes of existence must be different, since the time of existence in potentiality is different from the time of existence in actuality. This is something that Scripture does not mention explicitly, but rather states its very opposite; namely that He knows the created things when they are created; as the Almighty says: "Not a leaf falls but He knows it; and there is no grain in the dark bowels of the earth, nor anything green or dry, but is [recorded] in a clear Book."[3] Thus it must be laid down in religion that He knows that the thing, before it comes to be, [will be, and He knows that the thing, which has existed][4] has existed, and knows that what has decayed has decayed at the time of its decaying. This is what the basic principles of religion stipulate, due to the fact that ordinary people do not understand from the visible world other than this meaning.

As for the Mutakallimun, they do not possess a proof necessitating that [the Artisan] has another attribute; they only claim that the knowledge that changes with changing entities is created. Now no accidents inhere in the Glorious Originator, because, as they claim, what cannot exist apart from accidents must be created. We have already shown the falsity of this claim. Accordingly, it is necessary to accept this rule as it stands, and it must not be said that He knows the creation of what is created and the corruption of what is corrupted either with a created knowledge or with an eternal knowledge. [Such a claim] is an innovation in Islam: "Your Lord is never forgetful."[5]

---

3. Qur'an 6: 59.
4. Deleted in "B".
5. Qur'an 19: 64. In "A" there is the following addition: "What one should tell the select few is that eternal knowledge is not similar to created knowledge. For eternal knowledge encompasses all the sciences because denying Him knowledge of what He creates in these

As for the attribute of life, its existence follows necessarily from the attribute of knowledge, because it is apparent in the visible world that life is a precondition of knowledge. The Mutakallimun have maintained rightly that in the case of preconditions, one should be able to pass from the seen to the unseen.

162   With respect to the attribute of will, it is evident that He is characterized by it, since it is a precondition of the existence of something created by a knowing agent that he has willed it. Likewise, it is a precondition that [he] possess power. It is an innovation, however, to say that He wills the created things through an eternal will, and is equally something incomprehensible to the learned and unconvincing to the general public; by which I mean those who have attained the level of dialectic. Rather it must be said that He wills the existence of the thing at the time of its existence, and He does not will its existence at a time different from the time of its existence; as the Almighty says: "Indeed, when We want a thing to be, We just say to it: "Be", and it comes to be."[6] We reiterate that there is nothing to compel the common people to say that He wills the created things through an eternal will, except what the Mutakallimun alleged, namely that that in which accidents inhere is created.

* * *

However, if it is asked on what basis is speech attributed to Him, [we answer that it is attributed to Him][7] by virtue of His possessing the attributes of knowledge and the power to invent. For speech is nothing more than the speaker's performance of an act to convey to the addressed person the knowledge that is within him [or the addressed person being in a position whereby the knowledge that [the speaker] has is revealed to him][8], and this is one of the many actions that the speaker can perform. If the creature who is not a real agent (the human being), is capable of

three types of objects is absurd. Thus, it is certain that the Glorious One knows these objects, even though the modality of this knowledge is unknown, since that modality necessitates that eternal knowledge be analogous to created knowledge."

6. Qur'an 16: 40.
7. Deleted in "B".
8. Deleted in "B".

performing this sort of action by virtue of his knowledge and power, it is much more fitting that this should be necessarily the case with respect to the Real Agent. There is, moreover, another condition for this sort of action in the visible world: namely that it should be performed through an 163 intermediary which is speech. If this is the case, then it must be an action of God Almighty upon the soul of whomever He chooses from His servants through some intermediary; although it need not be a verbal one, which is still created by Him. For instance, it might be by the intermediary of an angel or by a revelation; that is without an utterance [which He creates. Instead, He might influence the listener in such a way that this meaning is disclosed to him, or it might be through an utterance][9] which God casts in the hearing of the person favored by the speech of the Almighty. It is to these three cases which the saying of the Almighty refers: "It is not given to any mortal that Allah should speak to him, except by revelation or from behind a veil. Otherwise, He sends forth a messenger who reveals by His permission whatever He wishes. [He is, indeed, All-High, All-Wise.]"[10] Revelation, then, is the creation of that meaning in the soul of the person receiving it without the intermediary of utterances created by [Him], or the disclosure of that meaning [of the utterance] to [him] through some action He performs in the soul of the addressed person; as the Almighty says: "Coming thus within two bows' length or closer. Then He revealed to His servant what He revealed."[11] And "from behind a veil" refers to the speech that takes place through utterances created by [God][12] in the soul[13] of the one He favors with His speech. This is the real speech, and it is the one that God favored Moses with. For this reason, the Almighty says: "Allah spoke to Moses directly."[14] As for His saying: "Otherwise, He sends forth a messenger",[15] it is the third way that occurs through the intermediary of an angel. God's speech might also include that which He imparts to the learned who are the heirs

9. Deleted in "A".
10. Qur'an 42: 50.
11. Qur'an 53: 9–10.
12. Deleted in "S".
13. In "A": *the hearing.*
14. Qur'an 4: 164.
15. In "A" *"who reveals".*

of the prophets through the intermediary of demonstrations. From this perspective, it is established among the learned that the Qur'an is God's speech.

It will thus have become evident to you that the Qur'an, which is the speech of God, is eternal, but that the words denoting it are created by God Almighty, not by men. In this respect the words of the Qur'an differ from the words used elsewhere other than in the Qur'an; I mean, the latter words are our own work with God's permission, whereas the words of the Qur'an are created by God. Whoever fails to understand this point in this way, fails to understand also this form [of the question]; nor can he understand how it can be said that the Qur'an is God's speech. As for the

164 letters of the written *Book*,[16] they are our own work, with God's permission. However, one should glorify them because they refer to the words created by God and to the meaning that is not created. Now whoever looks at words apart from meaning and does not distinguish the two, would maintain that the Qur'an is created; but those who look at the meaning of the words would say that the [Qur'an] is not created. The truth, however, consists in combining the two views.

The Ash'arites have denied that the speaker is the author of speech because they imagined that, if they accepted this principle, they would have to admit that God is the creator of His own speech. Having also believed that the speaker is the one in whom the speech subsists, they thought that they would be required, on the basis of these two principles, to say that God creates His speech in Himself, thereby rendering God Himself a bearer of accidents. That is why they maintained that the speaker is not the author of speech and that [God's] speech is but an eternal attribute of Himself, like knowledge and the other attributes. This claim, however, is true of inner speech, but not of the speech that indicates what is within the self, namely the utterances.

Believing that speech is an act of the speaker, the Mu'tazilites, by contrast, have claimed that speech is the utterance only. For this reason, they maintained that the Qur'an is created. The utterance, in their view, is an action, and as such it is not necessary that it should subsist in the

16. *Al-Muṣḥaf.*

speaker; whereas the Ash'arites insist on maintaining that the utterance must subsist in the speaker. In fact, in the visible world, this is true in both types of speech; the inner speech and the utterance denoting it. With respect to the Creator, however, inner speech is what subsists in Him; [what] denotes it does not subsist in Him. Thus, when the Ash'arites laid down as a condition that speech subsists absolutely in the speaker, they denied that the speaker is the agent of speech absolutely. By contrast, when the Mu'tazilites laid down as a condition that the speaker is absolutely the agent of speech, they denied the inner speech of the self. However, there is in the position of each one of the two sects a portion of truth and a portion of falsehood, as appears to you from our foregoing discourse.

* * *

165 As for the two attributes of hearing and vision, [Scripture has attributed them to God Almighty, on the ground that hearing and vision][17] pertain to certain apprehended notions in existing things that are not apprehended by the intellect. Now, since it is a precondition that the artisan apprehend everything in the artifact, he must possess these two [modes of] apprehension. It is necessary, then, that He should know [the objects] apprehended by sight and hearing, since they are made by him. Thus, all these point to the fact that, religiously speaking, the Glorious Creator possesses them; in so far as Scripture refers to His possessing knowledge. On the whole, from the meaning of the name of God and the object of worship, it should be clear that He apprehends through all modes of apprehension. For it would be futile for a human being to worship someone who does not apprehend that He is being worshiped; as the Almighty says: "Father, why do you worship that which neither sees nor hears, and can do nothing to help you?"[18] The Almighty says also: "Do you, then, worship, besides Allah, what does not profit or harm you a whit?"[19] This much of what God Almighty is characterized with and called by Scripture has commanded that the general public should know and nothing else.

* * *

17. Deleted in "B".
18. Qur'an 19: 42.
19. Qur'an 21: 66.

Of the innovations that sprang up around this issue is the question regarding these attributes: "Are they identical with the essence or additional to it; that is, are they intrinsic or nominal?" By "intrinsic" I mean attributes that describe the entity as such, not because of an additional meaning of the entity itself, as when we say "one and eternal". By "nominal" I mean attributes that describe the self on the basis of some notion subsisting in it. The Ash'arites call these attributes nominal, meaning that these attributes are extraneous to the entity, meaning that [God] knows and that His knowledge is extraneous to Himself, and that He is living, but life is additional to Himself, as is the case with visible [entities]. From this they are compelled to conclude that the Creator is a body, because then we would have an attribute and a substantive, a subject and a predicate, since this is the case with bodies. They must, then, 166 concede that the entity is self-subsistent and the attributes subsist in it; or else that each one of [the attributes] is self-subsistent, and thus the gods are many. This is the position of the Christians who believe in a Trinity of three Persons: Existence, Life and Knowledge. Regarding this the Almighty says: "Unbelievers too are those who have said that Allah is the third of three."[20] However, if they[21] hold that one of the two[22] subsists in itself and the other subsists in that which subsists in itself, then they would have to assume that it is a substance and an accident, since the substance is that which subsists in itself, whereas the accident subsists in something else. Now what is composed of substance and accident must necessarily be a body.

Similarly the statement of the Mu'tazilites, with respect to this response that the self and the attributes are identical, is very far from being part of primary notions,[23] but may be thought to be the opposite of that. For it might be thought that it is part of primary notions that what is known must be other than the knower and that it is not possible for what is known to be identical with the knower, except where the two terms of the relation are correlative, as when the father and the son refer to the

---

20. Qur'an 5: 73.
21. The Ash'arites.
22. The entity and the attributes.
23. Primary notions are the first concepts, or principles, of knowledge.

same denotation. However, this sort of instruction is beyond the comprehension of the general public, and its disclosure [to them] is heresy. It is more likely to misguide the ordinary people than to guide them rightly. Besides, the Mu'tazilites do not possess a proof to show that this is necessarily the case with respect to the First Being, glory be to Him, since neither they nor the Mutakallimun in general possess a proof denying the corporeality of [God], seeing that their denial of corporeality is based, for them, on the necessity of the created character of the body *qua* body. But we have shown in the first part of this book that they do not have a proof of this [and that those who have a proof of it][24] are the learned.

From this standpoint the Christians also erred. For they believed in the multiplicity of attributes and in their being substances not subsisting in something else but rather self-subsistent, just as the self itself. Furthermore, they believed that attributes of this kind are two: knowledge and life. In one respect they claimed that God is one, and 167 from another three; meaning that He is three with respect to existing, living and knowing, but One with respect to the fact that their sum-total is one thing.

We have here, then, three doctrines: (1) the doctrine of those who think that [the attributes] are identical with the self and there is no multiplicity therein, (2) the doctrine of those who admit multiplicity. The latter are divided into two groups: one regards multiplicity as self-subsistent[25], and the other regards it as multiplicity subsisting in something else[26]. However, all this is far from the intention of Scripture. If this is the case, then, what the ordinary people should know with regard to these attributes is only what Scripture discloses, which is the admission of their existence, without any further details. For it is not possible for the ordinary people to arrive at certainty on this issue in the first place. (By the ordinary people here, I mean all those who do not devote themselves to the demonstrative arts, whether they be those who have succeeded in acquiring the art of theology or not.) For it is not in the power of the art of

24. Deleted in "B".
25. This should be the second group.
26. This should be the third group. Ibn Rushd leaves out mentioning the third group.

theology (*Kalam*) to attain this measure of knowledge, since the highest grade of the art of *Kalam* is the attainment of dialectical, and not demonstrative, wisdom. Nor is it within the power of dialectic to arrive at the truth on this point.

From this discussion it has become evident what measure of knowledge [Scripture] has disclosed to the general public and the methods through which it led them to it.[27]

---

27. In "A" there is the following addition of: "The methods that the people have followed in these matters, claiming that they are part of the principles of religion, are not part of the principles of religion, but rather of what religion has remained silent about."

4

On the knowledge of
Transcendence

So far we have discussed in this book[1] the methods which religion has followed, firstly in teaching people about the existence of the Glorious Creator, secondly in denying the existence of a partner with Him, and thirdly in knowing His attributes. We have also discussed the measure which religion has determined expressly in each of these cases. Indeed, it is the measure, which, [if][2] added to, subtracted from, altered or interpreted allegorically, the happiness common to all mankind could not be attained. It remains for us to inquire into the methods through which [religion] has led people to exalt the Glorious Creator above all imperfections, the extent to which it made its position explicit regarding the exaltation, and the reason for which it has limited the people to that extent. Subsequently, we will discuss the methods whereby religion has led people to know [God's] actions and the extent of its help in this respect. Once we have done this we will have achieved the goal we set ourselves.

As for the knowledge of exalting and hallowing God, it is explicitly stated in more than one verse of the Precious Book. The most telling and complete one is the saying of the Almighty that "Nothing is like unto Him; He is the All-Hearing and the All-Seeing,"[3] as well as His saying:

---

1. As in Müller, *Philosophie und Theologie von Averroes.*
2. As in "A" only.
3. Qur'an 42: 11.

"Now, is He who creates like him who does not create? [Do you not take heed?]"[4] [The first verse is a conclusion, but the second verse is demonstrative; the saying of the Almighty "Now, is He who creates like him who does not create?" is a proof of His saying, "Nothing is like unto Him".][5] For it is ingrained in the natures of all mankind that the Creator must either possess an attribute not possessed by the one who does not create anything, [or possess an attribute unlike that possessed by the one

169 who does not create anything].[6] Otherwise the one who creates would not be a creator. If to this principle is added that the creature is not a creator, it follows that the attributes of the creature are either negated of the Creator, or exist in the Creator in a different manner from that in which they belong to the creature. We say in a different manner, because the attributes that belong to the Creator are attributes that we have inferred from those attributes found in the noblest of creatures on earth (namely man), such as affirming knowledge, life, power, will, and so on of Him. This is the meaning of the saying of the Prophet, peace be upon him, "God created Adam in His own image."

If it is established that Scripture has expressly asserted the negation of the similarity between the Creator and the creature and offered the proof necessitating that, and if the negation of the similarity is understood in two ways – the one being that the Creator does not possess many of the attributes of the creature, and the second that the attributes of the creature exist in Him in a more perfect and complete manner than the human mind can possibly comprehend – then let us consider what Scripture has expressly stated regarding these two manners, what it has remained silent about, and what was the wisdom of its reason for remaining [so] silent. We hold that, regarding Scripture's explicit negation of the creature's qualities of [God], it is obvious that it refers to the attributes of imperfection, such as death (as in the saying of the Almighty: "Put your trust in the Living God who does not die"[7]), sleep, and what falls short of it involving inattentiveness, dullness of perception, and failure to remember things.

4. Qur'an 16: 17.
5. Added in "A".
6. Deleted in "B".
7. Qur'an 25: 58.

All this is expressed in the saying of the Almighty: "Neither slumber nor sleep overtakes Him."[8] Of [these defects] also are forgetfulness and error, as He says: "['The knowledge thereof is with my Lord][9] in a Book. My Lord neither errs nor forgets.'"[10] Understanding the meaning of the negation of these imperfections is very close to necessary knowledge. For what part of [these imperfections] is close to necessary knowledge is what has been expressly denied of God Almighty by Scripture, whereas what was far from necessary primary cognitions, Scripture has indicated by stating that it is part of the knowledge of the fewest people, as the Almighty says in more than one verse of the Book: "But most people do not know," [which is part of] His saying: "Surely, the creation of the heavens and the earth is greater than the creation of mankind, but most people do not know,"[11] and His saying: "It is the original nature according to which Allah fashioned mankind. There is no altering Allah's creation. That is the true religion; but most people do not know."[12] If it is asked: "what is the proof (that is, the religious proof) for denying these imperfections of [God]?" we would answer that the proof is the fact that existing beings continue to be preserved without disruption or corruption. Now were the Creator liable to be overtaken by inattentiveness, error, forgetfulness or distraction, then existing beings would be disrupted. God Almighty has indicated this notion in more than one verse of His Book saying: "Allah holds the heavens and the earth firmly, lest they become displaced [were they displaced, none will hold them together after Him]. He is indeed Clement, All-Forgiving."[13] He also says: "[His throne encompasses the heavens and the earth,] and their preservation does not burden Him. He is the Exalted, the Great."[14]

On the Attribute of Corporeality

If it is asked: "What do you say regarding the attribute of corporeality? Is it one of the attributes which was explicitly denied by Scripture or one of

8. Qur'an 2: 255.
9. Deleted in "S".
10. Qur'an 20: 52.
11. Qur'an 40: 57.
12. Qur'an 30: 30.
13. Qur'an 35: 41.
14. Qur'an 2: 255.

those [attributes] on which it has remained silent?" We would answer that
it is evident from what we know of Scripture that it is one of the attributes
about which it has remained silent [although it is closer to being explicitly
mentioned in Scripture rather than denied].[15] For Scripture mentions the
face and the hands [of God] in more than one verse of the Precious Book.
Such verses give the impression that corporeality is one of the attributes
in which the Creator has surpassed the creature, in much the same way as
He has surpassed him with respect to the attributes of power, will and
other attributes which are common to the Creator and the creature,
although they exist more perfectly in the Creator. For this reason, many
171 people in Islam have come to believe that the Creator is a body unlike all
other bodies, such as the Hanbalites and many of their followers.

The rule with respect to this attribute [of corporeality], in my view, is
to follow the method used by Scripture, and assert neither its negation nor
affirmation. If somebody of the general public should ask about it, he
should be answered by reference to the saying of the Almighty: "Nothing
is like unto Him; He is the All-Hearing, the All-Seeing."[16]

He should also be dissuaded from raising such a question for three
reasons. First, understanding this notion is not close to what is self-
evident, either by one, two or even three degrees. You will ascertain this
yourself from the method followed by the Mutakallimun. For they have
claimed that the proof that He is not a body is that every such body is
created. If they are asked about the basis for their concluding that every
such body is created, they resort to the method that we mentioned earlier
regarding the creation of accidents and the fact that what cannot be
divested of accidents is created. It has become clear to you from our
discussion that this method is not demonstrative, and even if it were
demonstrative, it is not part of the nature of the majority of the public to
grasp it. Furthermore, those who maintain that the Glorious One consists
of an entity and attributes added to that entity actually stipulate thereby
that He is a body, more than they deny Him corporeality, as evidenced by
their negation of createdness of Him. This is, then, the first reason why
Scripture did not mention that He is not a body.

15. Deleted in "A".
16. Qur'an 42: 10.

The second reason is that the public believes that what exists is either the imaginable or sensible, and that what is neither imaginable nor sensible is non-existent. Thus, if they are told that there is an existing being which is not a body, their imagination would fail them and they 172 would consider it not-existent, especially if they are told that he is neither outside the world nor inside it, neither above it nor below it. For this reason the sect which affirmed corporeality considered the one which denied it minimalist[17], whereas the sect which denied corporeality considered the one affirming it maximalist.

The third reason is that, if the negation of corporeality were asserted explicitly, innumerable doubts would arise about it in religion similar to what is asserted with respect to the survival after death and the like. One such doubt arises regarding vision that was taught by the accredited Tradition.[18] For those who assert the negation [of corporeality] are two groups: the Mu'tazilites and the Ash'arites. As for the Mu'tazilites, this belief led them to deny the vision [of God]. By contrast, the Ash'arites wanted to combine the two beliefs; but when they found it difficult, they resorted, in their attempt to combine[19], to sophistical arguments, the weaknesses of which we shall show when we come to the discussion of the question of vision. [One of these arguments] is that the negation of direction with respect to the Glorious Creator entails at first sight that He is not a body, which leads to the ambiguity of religion. For the sending forth of prophets is based on the fact that revelation comes down to them from heaven, and on this [thesis] our religion is based; indeed our Precious Book came down from heaven, as the Almighty says: "We have sent it down on a blessed night."[20] Hence, the sending of revelation down from heaven is based on the belief that God is in heaven and that the angels come down from heaven and ascend to it, as the Almighty says: "Unto Him good words ascend and the righteous deed uplifts it."[21] The Almighty also says: "Unto Him the angels and the Spirit

17. The term in Arabic is *Mūlshi'a* which denotes reductionism. The opposite term is *Mukthira* or maximalism or pluralism.
18. *Al-Sunna.*
19. As eclectics are prone to do.
20. Qur'an 44: 2.
21. Qur'an 35: 10.

ascend."[22] Add to this all the things that compel those who deny direction, as we will show later when we speak of direction.

Another [argument] is that if one were to assert the denial of corporeality, one would have to assert also the denial of motion. But if one were to affirm the denial [of motion], it would be difficult to explain what was said regarding resurrection, to the effect that the Creator will rise up to the resurrected people and will take charge of judging them, as the Almighty says: "And your Lord comes, together with the angels in rows 173 upon rows."[23] Similarly it becomes difficult to interpret the famous Tradition (*Ḥadīth*) regarding the descent of revelation, even though interpretation is more appropriate to it than regarding resurrection, although what was said about revelation was repeatedly confirmed in Scripture.

Thus, one must not divulge to the general public what leads them to repudiate such [explicit statements] because their impact on the souls of the general public lies in clinging to their apparent meaning. However, if they are interpreted, one of two things would happen: either that interpretation would be applied to these and all similar statements in Scripture, in which case religion in its entirety would be torn apart and the wisdom intended by it would be lost; or they would all be accepted as part of what is ambiguous.[24] [All this would amount to the repudiation of religion and its eradication from the souls of people, without the advocate of such a view becoming aware of the catastrophic damage that he wreaks on religion.][25] Nonetheless, if you were to study the arguments that the proponents of interpretation in these matters resort to, you will find them all to be non-demonstrative. In fact the explicit religious statements are more convincing than these; I mean they are more believable. You will be able to ascertain this from our discussion of the proof upon which they based their repudiation of [corporeality. This has also been shown in the proof upon which they base their repudiation of][26] direction, as we will show later.

22. Qur'an 70: 4.
23. Qur'an 89: 22.
24. The reference is to Qur'an 3: 6 which distinguishes between ambiguous and non-ambiguous (or sound) verses.
25. Deleted in "A".
26. Deleted in "B".

What might lead you to recognize that Scripture did not intend to expressly repudiate this attribute [of corporeality] of God [as far as the general public is concerned, regarding their denial of this attribute][27] of the soul, is the fact that Scripture did not expressly disclose to the public what the soul is. The Precious Book says: "And they ask you about the spirit. Say: 'The spirit is of my Lord's command, and you have not been given except a little knowledge.'"[28] For it is difficult for the general public to conceive of a proof of the existence of a being that is self-subsistent, but is not a body. If the general public could comprehend the denial of this attribute, then Al-Khalil [Abraham], God's blessing and peace be upon him, would have been satisfied with it in his dispute with the unbeliever, when he said to him: "'My Lord is He who gives life and causes death,' 174 whereupon the other said: 'I give life and cause death'" and so on.[29] For Abraham could then have said: "You are a body, but God is not a body, because every body is created, as the Ash'arites would say. Likewise Moses, God's peace on him, would have been content with this in his debate with the Pharaoh, who claimed divinity. Similarly the Prophet, God's blessing and peace be upon him, would have been satisfied, in the case of the [One-eyed] Imposter, with directing the faithful to see the lie in his claim of divinity, [by saying] that [the Imposter] is a body whereas God is not a body. Instead [the Prophet], peace be upon him, said [in leading the believers to perceive the lie in the Imposter's claim of divinity]:[30] "your God is not one-eyed". He was content to show his lie by pointing to the existence of a defect,[31] which everyone would admit on the basis of one's rational intuition to be inadmissible in the case of the Glorious Creator.

Thus, as you see, all these are recent innovations in Islam. They are the cause of the appearance of many sects into which the Apostle predicted his community would splinter.

27. Deleted in "B".
28. Qur'an 17: 85.
29. Qur'an 2: 258. The rest of the passage is: "'Allah brings the sun from the East, brings it up from the West.' Thereupon the unbeliever was confounded. Allah does not guide the wrongdoers."
30. This addition exists only in "S".
31. His being one-eyed.

If someone were to say: "Seeing that religion does not expressly state either that God is or is not a body, how are we to answer the one who asks what He is?" This is a legitimate question and one cannot help but raise it. That is why it would not convince the general public to be told regarding a certain being whose existence they already concede, that it has no essence, because what has no essence has no identity.

In response, we would say that they[32] must be given the religious answer and be told that [God] is light. For it is the attribute that God described Himself with in the Precious Book, on the same ground that a thing is described by the property that is identical with itself; thus the Almighty says: "Allah is the light of the heavens and the earth."[33] With this description the Prophet, God's blessing and peace be upon him, has described Him in an accredited Tradition (*Hadith*). It is reported that he was asked, God's peace on him: "Have you seen your Lord?" He said "As a light I see Him." Moreover, in the *Isrā' Hadith* [or *The Prophetic Ascent* Tradition] it is stated that when he, God's blessing and peace be upon him, got closer to the Lotus Tree in the Seventh Heaven (*Sūdrat al-Muntaha*) that tree was covered with such a dazzling light that his sight was barred from seeing it or Him.

175   It is stated in the *Collection of Muslim*[34] that "there is a veil of light around God, were it to be lifted, the face of anyone looking at Him would be burnt." In some versions this *Hadith* speaks of "seventy veils of light." You should also know that this analogy is very appropriate to the Glorious Creator because [it][35] combines the claim that He is perceptible – though the eyes are incapable of perceiving Him – and intelligible – even though *He is not a body.* The existent,[36] for the general public, is that which is perceptible, whereas what is non-existent, according to them, is the imperceptible. Furthermore, since light is the noblest of all existing things, it is necessary to represent to them the noblest of all beings by it. There is also another reason why He should be called light. The mode of His existence, for the learned, who are well-grounded in knowledge, when

32. The general public or common people.
33. Qur'an 24: 35.
34. Author of an accredited collection of Prophetic Traditions (*Hadiths*), known as *Sahih Muslim.*
35. Deleted in "A".
36. In "S" and Müller: *existence.*

conceiving Him with their minds, is similar to the mode of the eyes looking at the sun, or rather like the eyes of the bats. This sort of description is appropriate to both classes of people and rightly so. Moreover, because God Almighty is the cause of existing entities and the cause of our perceiving them, just as the light has this characteristic with respect to colors (by which I mean that it is both the cause of the actual existence of colors and of our perception of them), it is fitting that God Almighty should call Himself light. And if it is admitted that He is light, then there can be no doubt regarding the vision which would occur at the Appointed Hour.

Thus the original belief prevalent in this religion regarding this attribute [of corporeality] and the innovations that arose concerning it will have become clear to you from this discussion. The reason why Scripture has remained silent about this attribute is that no one would admit the existence in the invisible world of a being who is not a body except one who apprehends demonstratively that there exists in the visible world an entity with this sort of attribute, namely the soul. However, since the knowledge of this aspect of the soul is not within the grasp of the general public, it was not possible for them to understand how there can be an entity which is not a body. When they were barred
176 from knowing the certainty,[37] we knew that they were barred from knowing this aspect of the Glorious Creator.

On Direction

As for the attribute of direction, it has been customary for people of [our] religion to affirm it of God Almighty since the beginning, until the Mu'tazilites denied it. Later on they were followed in this denial by the later Ash'arites, like Abū al-Ma'ālī[38] and his followers. Yet all the external references of Scripture require the affirmation of direction, such as the saying of the Almighty: "[And the angels shall be ranged around its borders,] eight of whom will be carrying above them, on that day, the Throne of your Lord,"[39] and His saying: "He manages the affair from the

37. In "A": *the soul.*
38. Al-Juwaynī, teacher of Al-Ghazālī (d. 1086).
39. Qur'an 69: 17.

heaven to the earth; then, it ascends to Him in one day whose measure is a thousand years of what you reckon."[40] There is similarly His saying: "Unto Him the angels and the Spirit ascend [on a day the duration thereof is fifty thousand years],"[41] and His saying: "Are you sure that He who is in heaven will not cause the earth to cave in upon you? Behold how it quakes!"[42] There are many other verses of this type, which, were one to interpret them, the whole of religion would become interpreted; whereas, if one were to declare them ambiguous, the whole of religion would become ambiguous. For all the religious laws are based on [the beliefs] that God is in heaven, wherefrom the angels bring down revelation to the prophets, that from heaven the holy books were sent down; and that to heaven the Prophet [Muḥammad], God's blessing and peace be upon him, was carried up during the midnight journey until he came close to the Lotus Tree.[43] Furthermore, all the philosophers are in agreement that God and the angels are in heaven, and all religions concur with them in this.

The difficulty which led those who deny direction to deny it is their belief that by admitting direction they are forced to admit place, and the 177 affirmation of place necessitates corporeality. We find none of these assertions necessary because direction is other than place. For direction refers: (1) either to the surfaces of the body itself which surround it and are six in number, and for which reason we say that the animal has above and below sides, right and left, a front and a rear, or (2) to surfaces of another body surrounding that body of six sides. The sides which are the surfaces of the body itself are not the place of the body itself, to begin with; whereas the surfaces of the bodies surrounding it constitute a place for it; as, for example, the surfaces of the air surrounding human beings, and the surfaces of the celestial sphere surrounding the surfaces of the air, constitute a place for the air. In like manner, the celestial spheres surround each other and constitute a place for one another. However, with respect to the surface of the outermost sphere, it has been proven that there is no such body outside it, for if this were the case, there would have

---

40. Qur'an 32: 5.
41. Qur'an 70: 4.
42. Qur'an 67: 16.
43. Reference to Prophet Muhammad's ascendance to heaven, called *al-Isra*ʾ.

to be another body outside this body, and the matter would go on *ad infinitum*. Therefore, the surface of the last body of the universe is not a place, to start with, since it is not possible for it to contain a body because every other place contains a body. Thus, if it can be proved that there is an existing entity on this side, it must be other than a body. Hence what is impossible there is the opposite of what these people thought (namely, a being which is a body, not a being which is not a body).

It is not open for these people to say that outside the universe there is the void, for in the theoretical sciences the impossibility of the void has been proven; what the word "void" denotes is nothing more than dimensions (i.e., length, width, height, and depth) within which there is no body. For were these dimensions removed, the void would become nothing; whereas, if the void were supposed to exist, it would be necessary for accidents to exist in no body. For, the dimensions are, doubtless, accidents in the category of quantity. However, it is known from the ancient and early beliefs and from preceding religions that that place[44] is the dwelling-place of spiritual entities (meaning God and the angels). However, that location is not a place nor is it encompassed by time, since all that is encompassed by space and time is corruptible. It follows, then, that what exists there must be incorruptible and ungenerable (*ghayra fasid wala kā'in*). This is evident from what I have just said. For since there is nothing [in this world] except this existing perceptible being or not-being, and since it is self-evident that the existing being is related to existence (it is said to exist or is in existence since it is impossible to say that it exists in not-being), then if there is [in the outer sphere] a being who is the noblest of all existing beings, it must be affiliated to the noblest part of the perceptible world, which is the heavens. Referring to the nobility of this part, the Almighty says: "Surely the creation of the heavens and earth is greater than the creation of mankind, but most people do not know."[45] All this is perfectly clear to the learned who are well-grounded in knowledge.

From this it will have become evident to you that positing direction is required by both religion and reason, and it is what religion teaches and is

178

---

44. Or the outermost heavenly sphere.
45. Qur'an 40: 57.

built upon. Thus, the repudiation of this rule entails the repudiation of religions. The difficulty in explaining this notion, while denying corporeality, is the absence of a parallel thereof in the visible world. This is precisely the reason why religion did not expressly deny the corporeality of the Glorious Creator, because the common people only assent to something pertaining to the invisible world when it is known to exist in the visible world, as is the case with knowledge. For since knowledge in the visible world is a precondition of the existence [of the knower], it is also a precondition of the existence of the invisible Artisan. However, when an assertion about the unseen is not known to the majority of people in the visible world, but only to those well-grounded in knowledge, religion either prohibits seeking its knowledge (especially where there is no need for the common people to know it, as in the case of the soul), or gives them representations of it from the world of experience, provided they need to know it for their own happiness, even if 179 representation is not the same as the matter intended for explanation, as in the many representations of resurrection.

The ordinary people do not discern the doubt inherent in the denial of direction, particularly since they are not told that God is not a body. Thus, in all this, one must follow the example of religion and refrain from interpreting what religion does not explicitly state should be interpreted.

With respect to these matters, as far as religion is concerned, people fall into three groups: (1) A group who is not aware of the doubts that arise concerning this matter, especially when these matters are accepted in their literal meaning in religion. (This group includes the majority of people who form the general public.) (2) Another group, having experienced these doubts, are unable to resolve them. These are superior to the public, but are inferior to the learned. This group is the one singled out for the allegation of ambiguity in Scripture, and God Almighty has reproached them.[46] By contrast, neither the learned nor the public finds any ambiguity in Scripture. It is in this sense that ambiguity should be understood. What happens to this group[47] of people with regard to

---

46. By this group, Ibn Rushd means the Mutakallimun. The third group is that of the philosophers or "people of demonstration" and is not explicitly mentioned in this passage.
47. The Mutakallimun.

religion is similar to what happens to the wheat bread, which is beneficial nourishment for the majority of bodies but might happen to be harmful to a minority of bodies, despite being beneficial to the majority. Similarly religious teaching is beneficial to the majority of people, but might be harmful to a minority, as is meant by the saying of the Almighty: "And by it, He leaves in error only the sinners."[48]

However, this occurs only with regard to a few verses of the Precious Book and to a minority of people. Most of these are verses which contain revelations about things in the invisible world for which there is no analogy in the visible world. In this case they are represented by examples of the closest and most similar things to them in the visible world. However, it happens sometimes that some people may mistake what is represented for the representation itself and thus become confused and perplexed. This is what is called "ambiguous" in Scripture but this sort of perplexity never affects the learned or the general public, who are really the only two classes of people, because they are healthy, and the proper food is suitable to the healthy bodies only. As for the others, they are the ill and those are the minority. For this reason the Almighty says: "As to those in whose hearts there is vacillation, they follow what is ambiguous in it, seeking sedition [and intending to interpret it]."[49] These are the adepts of dialectic (*Jadal*) and of theology (*Kalam*).

The worst that has befallen religion from this group of people is that they have interpreted many of [those passages] which they thought should not be understood literally, and maintained that such interpretation was not its intent; God made it look ambiguous in order to try and test His servants. We take refuge in God from entertaining this suspicion concerning Him. We rather hold that the Precious Book is miraculous in its clarity and eloquence. Hence, how far from the intent of Scripture are those who claim that what is not ambiguous is really ambiguous! Furthermore, they interpreted that which they alleged to be ambiguous telling everybody: "It is your duty to accept this interpretation." This is similar to what they claimed with respect to the verse referring to "the sitting on the Throne" and many other verses the apparent meaning of which they claimed to be ambiguous.

48. Qur'an 2: 26.
49. Qur'an 3: 6.

In short, then, it may be said that most of the interpretations that their advocates alleged to be the intent of Scripture, when examined carefully, are found to have no proof to support them, on the one hand; and they fail to have the effect of the literal meaning in appealing to the common people and influencing their conduct, on the other. The primary [purpose][50] of acquiring knowledge, where the common people are concerned, is to lead them to action, so that what is more useful in action is more worthy of pursuit. However, what is intended by knowledge, with respect to the learned, is both objectives, namely knowledge and action.

The case of the person who interprets a part of Scripture and claims that what he has interpreted is what Scripture has intended, and then divulges that interpretation to the common people, is similar to the case 181 of [someone] who takes a medication prepared by a skillful physician for the preservation of the health of all or most people. It may [then happen] that somebody took that very well-prepared medication without profiting from it, due to a bad humor which only affects a small minority of people. He then went on to claim that some of the ingredients that the original physician had prescribed in preparing that medication for the general benefit [of the public] were not intended for that medication habitually referred to by the name applied to it in that language, but were rather intended for another medication which may be referred to, through a remote metaphor, by the name of that medication. He has thus removed the original ingredients from that great medication, and replaced them with the ingredients that he believed the physician had intended, telling people: "This is [the medication] intended by the original physician." Thereupon people proceeded to use this medication prepared in the manner interpreted by that interpreter and thus the health of many people began to deteriorate because of it. When [others began] to feel the damage caused by this medication to the humor of so many people, they attempted to remedy it by replacing some of its ingredients with some ingredients other than the original ones, a new kind of disease, other than the original one, afflicted the people. Then a third person came forward offering an interpretation of the ingredients of the medication other than

50. Deleted in "B".

the first and the second interpretations. Thus a third kind of disease other than the first two kinds afflicted the people. A fourth [interpreter] then came forward offering an interpretation of the medication quite different from the previous interpretations, and a fourth kind of disease, other than the preceding diseases, afflicted the people. After the passage of a long period of time since the preparation of this great medication, and because many people had altered and changed its ingredients through a chain of interpretations, many diseases spread [in the community] and the common benefit intended was lost, as far as the majority of people for whose sake it was originally intended were concerned. This is the case with those nascent [sects][51] that use this method in matters of religion; for each group interprets Scripture in a way different from the way the other 182 sect interprets it, claiming that that, indeed, is the intent of the lawgiver. As a result, religion is utterly ripped apart and is completely displaced.

When the lawgiver, God's blessing and peace be upon him, saw that something like this was bound to happen with respect to his religion, he said: "My community shall split into seventy-two Sects, all but one shall be consigned to hell." He meant by that one the Sect that followed the literal meaning of Scripture and did not interpret it, divulging [its interpretations] to the public. Now if you were to ponder the state of this [our] religion at the present time and the widespread corruption it is exposed to due to interpretation, you would realize that this illustration is sound.

The first group to change this great medication were the Kharijites, followed by the Mu'tazilites, the Ash'arites and then the Sufis. Then Abū Hāmid [Al-Ghazāli] came and opened the flood-gates of the valley so that all the towns were swept away. For, he divulged all [the secrets of] philosophy to the general public, as well as the opinions of the philosophers, to the extent that he was able to understand them, in a book called *The Intentions of the Philosophers (Maqāṣid al-Falāsifah)*. He claimed that he wrote the book merely for the purpose of refuting them. Then he wrote his well-known book *The Incoherence of the Philosophers (Tahāfut al-Falāsifah)* exposing their unbelief (*Kufr*) with respect to three

51. As in "A".

questions wherein they violated the consensus [of the Muslim Community], as he claimed, and accusing them of innovation (*Bid'ah*)[52] with respect to other issues. He advanced in it many doubtful and perplexing arguments that drove many people away from both philosophy and religion. Then he said in his book known as *The Jewels of the Qur'an (Jawāhir al-Qur'an)* that what he wrote in *The Incoherence* were merely dialectical arguments, but the truth is to be found in his other book entitled *What Is Concealed From The Unworthy (Al-Madnūn bihi 'ala ghayri Ahlihi)*. Then he enumerated, in his well-known book *The Niche of Lights (Mishkāt al-Anwār)*, the various classes of people who know God truly, stating that most of them are sealed off from the knowledge of God, except for those who believe that God Almighty is other than the mover of the first heaven, and is the One from whom that mover has emanated. This is a clear admission on his part of subscribing to the doctrines of the philosophers in the metaphysical sciences. However, he had claimed in more than one place that their metaphysical sciences are conjectures, unlike the rest of their sciences.[53] Nevertheless, in his book, *The Deliverer from Error (Al-Mūnqidh minal-Dalāl)*, he reproached the philosophers, indicating that certain knowledge arises by means of withdrawal [from the world] and reflection only, and that this level of knowledge is equivalent to the levels of knowledge attained by the prophets. He reiterated the same [opinion] in his book, entitled *The Alchemy of Happiness (Kimiyā 'al-Sā'ādah)*. As a result of this confusion and muddling, people split into two groups, one who took it upon itself to denounce philosophy and the philosophers and the other to interpret Scripture and assimilate it to philosophy. However, all this is an error; for Scripture should be accepted on its face value and the harmony between religion and philosophy should not be divulged to the ordinary people because such divulgence amounts to divulging to them philosophical conclusions without providing them with any proof thereof. To divulge philosophical conclusions to people who do not possess the demonstrations thereof is neither lawful nor permissible because [those people] do not belong to

183

---

52. Or, *heresy.*
53. Meaning logic and mathematics, which Al-Ghazāli did not denounce, as he had done in the case of metaphysics and parts of physics.

the class of the learned, who combine religion and reason, nor the ordinary people who follow the literal meaning of Scripture. As a result of [Al-Ghazāli's] action some people violated the principles of both philosophy and religion, while others preserved them both. As for violating the principles of religion, it consists in his making public the interpretations that should not be made public; whereas his violation of the principles of philosophy consists in expressing opinions that should not be divulged except in books of demonstration.[54] As for his preserving both [philosophy and religion], it consists in the fact that many people do not find any contradiction between the two in the way they were brought

184 together. He emphasized this point by defining the manner of harmony between them in the book that he called *The Discrimination Between Islam and Heterodoxy (al-Tafriqah baynal-Islām wa'l-Zandaqah)*. In it he has enumerated the various kinds of interpretations, asserting categorically therein that the person who resorts to interpretation is not an unbeliever, even if he violates the consensus [of the Muslim Community] in his interpretations. Hence, what he did in this regard is harmful to religion in one respect, to philosophy in another respect, and to both of them in yet a third respect.[55] However, if one were to examine carefully what this man has done, it would appear that it is essentially harmful to both of them – philosophy and religion – although it could be accidentally useful to them both. Making philosophy public to those who are not worthy of it leads necessarily either to repudiating philosophy or repudiating religion. It might lead accidentally to bringing the two together.

The right course for him to follow would have been not to divulge philosophy to the general public, but once this divulgence was done, the right thing now was for that group of the public that believes that religion contradicts philosophy, to know that it does not contradict it. Similarly those among the philosophers who believe that philosophy contradicts religion, [should know that] it does not. Every adherent of the two groups should be told that he does not really know the essence of each one of them; neither the essence of religion nor the essence of philosophy. Thus, the opinion [of Al-Ghazāli] that religion contradicts philosophy, is either

54. Or *logic*.
55. In "A": *and beneficial to them in another respect.*

a heresy in religion, not a fundamental principle thereof, or a mistaken opinion in philosophy (by which I mean a mistaken interpretation thereof, as happened in the case of [God's knowledge of] particulars and similar questions). For this reason, we were forced in the present book to define the fundamental principles of religion. For, if its principles are carefully examined, they would be found to be more compatible with philosophy than its interpretations. The same is true of the opinion of those who believe that philosophy contradicts religion.[56] They should know that the reason is that they did not fully comprehend philosophy or religion. That is why we were compelled to write our book *The Decisive Treatise on the Harmony Between Philosophy and Religion (Faṣl al-Maqāl)*.[57]

185

The Problem of Vision

Seeing that this issue [of direction] has been explained, let us go back to where we were. What is left of this part of well-known questions for us to deal with in this section is the question of vision. It might be thought that this question is somehow part of the previous section, because the Almighty says: "Vision does not attain Him, but He attains the vision."[58] For this reason, the Muʻtazilites denied [vision] and rejected the references to it in religious traditions, despite their being numerous and well-known, and so they were held blameworthy on that account. The reason why this doubt arose in religion is that when the Muʻtazilites believed that God's corporeality should be denied, and that they must make this [denial] known to all those religiously responsible, it followed in their view that, if corporeality is denied, direction must be denied too; and if direction is denied, vision must be denied, since every visible object is to one side of the beholder or the other. Hence, they found themselves compelled for that reason to reject the transmitted religious traditions. They held that those traditions (*Hadiths*) have emanated from a singular source, and [thus] do not amount to necessary knowledge, since the literal meaning of the Qur'an contradicts them, as in the saying of the Almighty: "Vision does not attain Him."

56. In "A" there is the addition: in something.
57. Or *The Decisive Treatise on the Relation of Religion and Philosophy*.
58. Qur'an 6: 103. In Arberry's translation: "The eyes attain Him not, but He attains the eyes."

As for the Ash'arites, they sought to combine both beliefs: the denial of corporeality and the possibility of seeing through the senses that which is not a body. However, they found that too difficult, and thus they resorted to misleading sophistical arguments – arguments that give the impression of being sound arguments when, in fact, they are false. For, it is possible to find among arguments what is found among people; just as one may find among people the perfectly virtuous, those who are beneath that in virtue and those who pretend to be virtuous, when in fact they are not, but are hypocrites, the same is true of arguments. Some are completely certain, some are less than certain and some are disputatious arguments which
186 give the impression that they are certain when, in fact, they are false. The arguments that the Ash'arites advanced in connection with this issue are either refutations of the arguments of the Mu'tazilites, or arguments intended to prove the possibility of vision of something which is not a body, and to show that no absurdity would follow from such a supposition.

With respect to [the arguments with which] they challenged the Mu'tazilites, claiming that "everything visible must be to one side of the beholder", some have maintained that this is true in the case of the visible world but not that of the invisible world, and that this is not one of the cases wherein the status of the visible world could be extended to the invisible world. It is possible [they argued,] for a human being to see [that which is not to one side, provided it is possible for him to see][59], with the faculty of perception, without an eye. However, those people confused the apprehension of the intellect with eyesight[60] because the intellect apprehends what is not to one side; I mean, is in place. But it is evident that with respect to the perception of sight, one presupposes not only that the object seen be to one side, but also be to a specific side. For this reason, vision is not possible from whichever position the sight happens to be in, with respect to the object seen; it must rather be in a certain position and meet specific conditions too. These [conditions] are three: the presence of light, a transparent medium between the sight and the seen object,[61] and

59. Deleted in "B".
60. In "B" *the apprehension of sight*.
61. In Aristotelian physics, this is the diaphanous medium identified with ether. (Cf. *De anima* II, 418 b7.)

the seen object being necessarily colored. Rejecting these self-evident conditions with respect to vision amounts to a rejection of the primary principles known to all people by nature, and a repudiation of the sciences of optics and geometry. But those people, I mean, the Ash'arites, have maintained that one of the cases where the inference from the visible world could be extended to the invisible world is that of the precondition, as when we judge that every knower is living, since life appears in the visible world as a precondition for the existence of the knower. Our response to them is that, if this is the case, then it appears also that in the visible world these things are preconditions of seeing. Therefore, apply your own rule and treat the invisible world in this case as analogous to the visible world.

187

Abū Hāmid [Al-Ghazāli] has tried, in his book known as *The Intentions [of the Philosophers] (Maqāṣid [al-Falāsifah])*, to dispute this premise (namely that every visible object is to one side of the beholder), by [asserting that] the person sees himself in a mirror, without himself being to a side opposite to the side where he is. For, when he sees himself, and his self is not on the opposite side, he actually sees himself not to one side. But this is sophistry because what is seen is his shadow, and the shadow is to a given side, since the shadow is in the mirror, and the mirror is to a given side.

Of the arguments which [the Ash'arites] cited in support of the possibility of seeing what is not a body, they have two famous ones. Their most famous argument consists in their claim that a thing is seen either by virtue of being colored, by virtue of being a body, by virtue of being a color, or by virtue of being an existing entity. Sometimes they enumerate other aspects than these pertaining to the existing being;[62] then add that it is absurd that [something] should be seen by virtue of being a body. For if this were the case, it would not be possible for the color to be seen,[63] and it is also absurd for [the thing] to be seen by virtue of being a color, because if this were the case, then the body would not be seen. [They

---

62. In "A" *the existing ones.*
63. In "A" on page 59, there is this addition: "[It would not be possible] to see what is not a body. It is absurd that it can be seen *qua* colored, because if this were the case, then color would not be seen, and it is absurd to see, etc."

said][64] that if all these alternatives that could be imagined in this connection are false, then it only remains that the body is seen by virtue of being an existing entity. The fallacy in this claim, however, is obvious, because visible objects are either visible in themselves or are visible by virtue of that which is visible in itself. This is the case with colors and bodies. A color is visible in itself, whereas a body is visible by virtue of the color. For this reason what does not have a color cannot be seen. Were it possible for something to be seen merely by virtue of its existence, then it

188 would have been possible for sounds and the other five sensations to be seen. In that case, sight, hearing, and the rest of the five senses would be but one sense-organ; but all these suppositions are contrary to reason.

Due to the importance of this and similar questions, the Mutakallimun were forced to admit that it is possible for colors to be heard and sounds to be seen, but all this is unnatural and incomprehensible. For it is evident that the sense of sight is not the same as the sense of hearing and that the objects of the former are not the same as the latter. Furthermore, the organ of the one is not the same as the organ of the other: it is not possible for sight to become hearing, just as it is not possible for colors to become sounds. Those who claim that it is possible for sounds to be seen at a certain point should be asked: "What is sight?" Their answer must be that it is the faculty of perceiving visible objects, such as colors and the like. Then they could be asked, "What is hearing?" to which they must inevitably answer that it is the faculty of perceiving sounds. If they admit all this, then they could be asked further: "Is sight, when it perceives sounds, sight only, or hearing only?" If they answer hearing only, then they have admitted that it does not perceive colors, but if they answer sight only, then it does not perceive sounds. If it is neither merely sight, because it perceives sounds, nor hearing only, because it perceives colors, it is then both seeing and hearing. Accordingly all things would constitute one single entity, including opposites. I believe this is something admitted by the theologians of our religion[65], or something they are forced to admit. However, this is a sophistical opinion that was held by a famous group of ancient Sophists.

64. As in "S".
65. Al-Mutakallimun.

The second method that the Mutakallimun adopted in explaining the possibility of vision is the method favored by Abū al-Ma'āli in his book known as *The Guidance (Al-Irshād)*. It can be summarized as follows: the senses perceive the things themselves, but what distinguishes existing things from each other are states (*Aḥwāl*)[66] which are not things, and so the senses do not perceive them, but perceive the things themselves. The essence is the same as existence itself, common to all existing things. Thus, the senses perceive the thing in so far as it is an existing entity. All this is entirely false.

The clearest evidence for the falsity of this opinion is that if sight perceived things as such, it would not have been able to distinguish between black and white because things are not distinguished by virtue of that which they have in common. Nor would it have been possible in the case of the senses, either for sight to perceive different kinds of colors, or for hearing to perceive different kinds of sounds, or for taste to perceive different kinds of tastes. It would also have been necessary for all the percepts of sensible objects to be of one kind, so that there would be no difference between the percept of hearing and the percept of seeing. All this, however, is well beyond the grasp of human reason. In fact the senses perceive the things themselves that can be pointed to through the intermediary of their perception of the proper objects of sense. The point of the fallacy in this [position] is that what is perceived essentially has been mistaken for what is perceived in itself. Indeed had people not been familiar with these arguments and glorifying their exponents from birth, it would have been impossible to find in them any hint of conviction, nor would anyone with a sound natural disposition have assented to them.

The root-cause of this confusion that has affected religion (to the point that it forced its defenders, as they claim, to resort to such strange arguments, which are the object of derision for all those who have the slightest acquaintance with distinguishing the various forms of arguments) is the divulging of what neither God nor His Apostle permitted in religious matters; namely, the divulging of the denial of corporeality to the public. For, it is difficult to combine in the same mode of belief that

---

66. In Ash'arite theology, these states are modes of being, distinct from both the entity or accidents pertaining to it.

there is an existing entity who is not a body yet is visible to eyesight
because the perceptions of the senses are either bodies or in bodies. That
is why some people have held that vision is an added knowledge, at the
190 time [of vision]; but it is inappropriate to make this claim known to the
common people also. For since the intellects of the common people
cannot be rid of the influence of the imagination so that what they cannot
imagine does not exist for them, imagining what is not a body is
impossible and believing in the existence of what is not imaginable is
impossible, according to them, Scripture has avoided disclosing this
matter to them. Thus, it has ascribed to God Almighty, for their
information, certain attributes which are close to their faculty of
imagination, such as hearing, seeing, a face and the like. At the same
time it took care to tell them that He is unlike any imaginable existing
thing, neither does He resemble any existing thing.

Were the intention of [Scripture] to inform the masses that He is not a
body, it would not have mentioned anything of the kind. But since light is
the noblest of all imaginable things, it has likened Him to light, which, of
all existing things, is the most obvious to the faculties of sense and
imagination. It is also through such representations, that [the common
people] are able to understand the notions associated with survival after
death; by which I mean that those notions are represented to them in
terms of imaginable and sensible objects. Thus, when Scripture's attributes
of God Almighty are understood literally, neither this nor any similar
difficulty would arise. For, when it is asserted that God is light or that He
has a veil of light, as stated in the Qur'an and other accredited Traditions,
and when one is then informed that the faithful shall see Him in the
hereafter as they see the sun, there would not arise, either as regards the
common people or the learned, any doubt or difficulty. For it has been
demonstrated by the learned that that condition is one of added
knowledge. However, if divulged to the common people, they would
either renounce religion or regard those who divulge such views to them
as unbelievers. Thus, anyone who diverges from the right path of religion
in these matters has gone astray.

As for you, if you examine Scripture carefully, you will find that even
though it has illustrated these matters to the common people by

representations without which they could not have understood them, it
191 has alerted the learned to the real meaning of these matters, of which it
gave such representations to the common people. Thus, one must observe
the limits which religion has set with respect to the instruction it has
proposed for each class of people, and avoid mixing up the two kinds of
instruction, destroying thereby the religious and prophetic wisdom. That
is why [the Prophet,] God's peace be on him, said: "We, the prophets, have
been ordered to put people in their places, and to address them according
to their rational capacities." Now, whoever regards all mankind as being of
the same stripe, with respect to instruction, is similar to one who regards
them as being of the same stripe, with respect to certain actions; but all
this is contrary to what is both sensible and rational.

It will have become clear to you from this that vision [with respect to
God Almighty], is a literal notion and that no inconsistency should arise,
if Scripture is understood literally; I mean that if one does not openly
deny or affirm corporeality of God. Having understood the original
dogmas of religion regarding transcendence and the extent to which they
have gone in teaching the general public about this matter, it may be
appropriate to proceed to the part pertaining to the knowledge of the
actions of God Almighty. This will be the fifth chapter of this inquiry, and
with it we conclude the discussion of our intended subject.

5

On the knowledge of
God's actions

192 We only discuss in this chapter five questions that are the principles around which all this section revolves.

The first question: On proving that the world is created.

The second question: On commissioning Messengers.[1]

The third question: On God's decree and predestination.

The fourth question: On divine justice and injustice.

The fifth question: On resurrection.

I. The first question:[2] on the creation[3] of the world

193 You should know that what religion has intended with respect to the knowledge of the world, is that it is made by God Almighty and invented by Him and that it did not come to be by chance or by itself. Indeed the method[4] adopted by religion in leading people to accept this fundamental principle is not the method of the Ash'arites. We have already shown that that method is not one of the demonstrative methods proper to the learned, nor is it one of the general methods common to all mankind. The

---

1. *Apostles* or *prophets*
2. Deleted in "A".
3. Ibn Rushd uses the terms creation (*Ḥudūth*), using (*Sun'*) and origination (*Ījād*) interchangeably throughout this work.
4. In "A" *the methods.*

latter are the simple methods, in the sense that they have few simple premises and their conclusions are close to being self-evident propositions. However, explanations formulated according to complicated and elaborate syllogisms, based on diversified principles, are never used by Scripture in instructing the common people. Thus, whoever uses any other kind of methods – by which I mean simple methods for instructing the common people – and attributes them to Scripture, is ignorant of its intent and diverges from its path. Similarly Scripture does not introduce syllogisms in such matters, except when parallels are already found for them in the visible world. Whenever there is an urgent need for introducing the common people to a certain issue, Scripture represents it [to them] by reference to the closest things to it, as is the case with the nature of resurrection; whereas when it comes to that which the common people do not need to know, they are told that such knowledge does not belong to them, as the Almighty says regarding the spirit.[5]

Thus, if this principle is granted, it follows that the method employed by Scripture for instructing the general public about the creation of the world must be one of the simple methods acknowledged by everyone. However, since the creation [of the world] has nothing comparable to it in the visible world, it is necessary for Scripture to use for its representation [instances] drawn from the production of observable things.

As for the method which Scripture has adopted in teaching the common people that the world is made by God Almighty, it will be found, if one examines carefully the verses containing a reference to it, that that method is the method of providence, which is one of the [two] methods mentioned earlier as a proof of the existence of the Glorious Creator. For just as a certain person, upon seeing a sensible object and finding it made in a certain shape, of a certain measure, and in a position conducive altogether both to the advantage known to accrue from that sensible object and the end desired, is forced to admit that if that object were to exist in a different shape, or a different position, or a different measure, that advantage would not accrue from it, he would, then, know for certain that that object has a maker who made it and that it is for this reason that

---

5. Qur'an 17: 85.

its form, position, and measure came to be conducive to that advantage; and that it is not possible for the union of all these factors to be conducive to such advantage by accident. For example, if a person sees a stone lying on the ground and finds its shape suitable for sitting upon and finds its position and measure are similarly [suitable], he would conclude, then, that that [stone][6] was made by an artisan who gave it that position and put it in that place. If he does not find anything in it suitable for sitting, he would conclude definitely that its being in that place and its having a certain property is a matter of chance and no agent actually put it there.

The same is true of the world as a whole. For if a human being looks at what [it] contains in the form of the sun, moon, and other planets, which are 195 the causes of the four seasons, the day and the night, the rain, the water and the winds, how certain parts of the world are inhabited by people, together with different kinds of animals and plants; and if he looks at the earth and how it is suitable to the habitation of people and other wild animals, and how water is suitable for marine life, and the air for flying birds, and that if any part of this creation and structure were disturbed the existence of creatures herebelow would be disturbed, he would know for certain that it is impossible that this suitability of all the parts of the universe to mankind, animals, and plants is a matter of chance. It must rather be intended by an intending and willing Agent who is God Almighty. He would also conclude categorically that the world is created.[7] For he will know necessarily, then, that it would have been impossible for this suitability to exist, had the world not been the work of a Maker, but rather of chance.

That this sort of proof is both conclusive and simple is clear from what we have just said. For it is based on two principles admitted by all. The first is that the world with all its parts is suited to the existence of man and all existing entities [here below]. The second principle is that everything that is suited in all its parts to a certain action is one and directed towards a single purpose and is necessarily created. From these two principles it naturally follows that the world is made and has a Maker, for, the argument from providence entails both meanings, and for this reason it is the best argument for proving the existence of the Maker.

6. Deleted in "A".
7. Or *made*.

That this type of demonstration is the one found in the Precious Book is evident from more than one verse wherein the beginning of creation is mentioned. One such verse is the saying of the Almighty:

> "Have We not made the earth as a couch for you? And the mountains as pegs? [And created you in pairs? And made your sleep a period of rest? And made the night as a garment? And made the day a source of livelihood? And built above you seven mighty [heavens]? And created a shining lamp? And brought down from the rain-clouds abundant water?] To bring forth thereby grain and vegetation? And luxuriant gardens?"[8]

196 When these verses are studied carefully, one finds them drawing attention to the suitability of the various parts of the world to the existence of mankind. For He starts by pointing to something self-evident to us, human beings, whether black or white; namely that the earth is created in such a manner that it is possible for us to dwell in it. For were it movable,[9] had a form other than its present form, was in a position other than its actual position or of a magnitude other than its actual magnitude, it would not have been possible for us to exist or be created on it. All this is implied in His saying: "Have we not made the earth as a couch for you?" For the meaning of a couch combines agreement of the shape, rest, and position, in addition to that of comfort and softness. How wonderful is this miraculousness, how beautiful this metaphor, and how marvelous that combination! For the word "couch" has combined everything on earth, pertinent to its suitability to human habitation. The scientists are perfectly aware of this fact, as is shown in their lengthy discourses over extensive periods of time. God bestows His mercy on whomever He pleases.

However, the words of the Almighty "And the mountains as pegs?" alert us to the advantage of the stability of the earth, due to the existence of mountains. For if the earth were smaller than it is, say without any mountains, then it would have been rocked due to the movements of the other elements (i.e., water and air), and it would have quaked and become unhinged. Indeed were this the case then all animals would have

---

8. Qur'an 78: 6–7. As usual Ibn Rushd quotes the first and last parts of this passage only, with the rubric "from … to".

9. In Ptolemaic cosmology the earth was fixed as the center of the universe.

inevitably perished. Thus, the suitability of its stability to the entities existing on it did not arise by chance, but was produced by an intending and a willing Agent. Therefore, it is necessarily made by that intending Agent who determined it to possess those properties suitable for the existence of those existing entities on it.

[God] has also drawn our attention to the suitability of night and day to the existence of living beings, saying "And [We] made the night as a garment and the day a livelihood"[10], meaning that He made the night like a cover or clothing to protect existing entities here below from the heat of the sun. For if the sun did not set at night, then all the existing entities which depend on the sun for their life, like animals and plants, would have perished.[11] For, since the clothing might protect from heat, although it is a cover, and since the night has these two aspects, God has called it "a garment". This is one of the most beautiful metaphors. There is also another benefit to animals from the night; namely that it allows them to sleep soundly, due to the absence of light that moves the senses to the external parts of the body in a state of wakefulness. That is why the Almighty says: "And made your sleep a period of rest", that is, restful due to the darkness of the night. Then He says: "And built above you seven mighty [heavens], and created a shining lamp", indicating by the term "building" the notion of invention and that of craftiness, order, and organization. He also expressed by the notion of "might" the power with which He endowed [the heavens] to move without cessation or weariness. There is no fear also that [they] might collapse like ceilings and lofty edifices, as appears from His saying: "And We made the sky a well-guarded canopy." There is in all this an indication by Him of the suitability of [the heavens] with their numbers, shapes, positions, and motions to what exists here on earth and around it; so much so that if one of the heavenly bodies were to stop for a single moment, let alone all of them, everything on earth would perish. Some people have contended that the blowing of the Horn that causes the Seizure refers to the grinding of the celestial spheres to a halt.[12]

197

---

10. Qur'an 78: 5.
11. Ibn Rushd clearly means the setting of the sun as followed by its rising.
12. This is a reference to the blowing of the Horn on the Last Day by the angel.

The Almighty has also drawn our attention to the special benefit of the sun and its suitability to what exists on earth, saying: "And [We] created a shining lamp."[13] He called it "a lamp" because darkness is the
198 original state and light is adventitious in relation to darkness, just as the lamp is adventitious in relation to the darkness of the night. Were it not for the lamp, mankind would not have benefited from the sense of sight at night. Similarly, were it not for the sun animals would not have benefited from this sense of sight to begin with. The Almighty has drawn our attention to this benefit of the sun, but not its other benefits, because it is the noblest and most manifest of them all. He has also indicated the aforementioned providential advantage of rain for the nourishment of animals and plants and the fact that it falls in certain amounts and at certain times, suited to the growth of vegetation, which cannot be the product of chance, but must be the product of providential care for everything here below. Thus the Almighty says: "And we brought down from the rainclouds abundant water to bring forth thereby grain and vegetation, and luxuriant gardens."

The verses in the Qur'an that draw our attention to this notion are numerous, such as: "Do you not see how He created for you seven heavens superposed upon one another? And placed the moon therein as a light and made the sun as a lamp? And Allah caused you [plants] to grow out of the earth?"[14] as well as His saying: "Who has made the earth a couch for you, and the heavens a canopy."[15] Indeed, if we were to enumerate all such verses, detailing how they alert us to the presence of that providence which points to the Creator and the creation, many volumes would not suffice. This is not our intention in this book. Perhaps, if God prolongs our life, and we have enough free time, we might write a book on the providence to which the Precious Book has drawn attention.[16]

You should also know that this type of demonstration is the very opposite of the demonstration that the Ash'arites regarded as the proper method leading to the knowledge of God Almighty. They have claimed

13. Qur'an 78: 13.
14. Qur'an 71: 15–17. God caused plants to grow for your sustenance.
15. Qur'an 2: 22.
16. No such book appears to have been written by Ibn Rushd.

that existing things point to God Almighty, not due to any wisdom
199 inherent in them and necessitating providence, but rather due to mere
contingency, due to the fact that what appears in all existing entities as
possible in reason may be of this type or its opposite. However, if this
possibility is even then there would be no wisdom [in creation], and there
would be no correspondence, to begin with, between mankind and other
parts of the world. For were it possible, as they claim, for all the existing
entities to be other than what they are, just as easily as they actually are,
then there would be no correspondence between mankind and the
existing things, with whose creation God has favored man and
commanded him to thank Him for. What this opinion entails is that the
possibility of His creating man as part of this world is equivalent to the
possibility of creating him, for instance, in the void, which they believe
exists. Indeed for them it is possible for man to be of a different shape and
a different constitution, and still act like a human being! It is also possible,
in their view, that he may be part of another world entirely different from
this world in definition and detail, in which case there would be no grace
for which man should be thankful. For that which is not necessary or is not
the most fitting for man's existence, man can certainly dispense with, and
that which man can dispense with does not count as a grace he is favored
with. All this is contrary to human nature.

On the whole, just as one who denies that in manufactured things the
effects are ordered according to appropriate causes, or is unable to
understand this fact, does not have much knowledge of the making or the
Maker, similarly, the one who denies that the effects are ordered
according to causes in this world must deny[17] the existence of the Wise
Maker, may He be exalted beyond measure.

Their[18] claim that God has decreed that habit should govern these
causes, and that they do not affect the effects, by His leave, is a claim far
removed from the dictates of wisdom. In fact it destroys wisdom, because
200 if these effects could exist [without these causes, just as they could exist][19]
with them; then what wisdom is there in their existence through these

17. In "A" there is the addition, *The art and wisdom; and whoever denies art and wisdom must deny* etc.
18. The Ash'arites.
19. Deleted in "B".

causes? For the existence of the effects through causes may take one of three forms:

1. Either the existence of causes for the sake of the effects is a matter of necessity, like man's being in need of nourishment;
2. or they are for the sake of what is best; that is, the effects will be better and more perfect thereby, as is the case of man having two eyes;
3. or that they are neither for the sake of what is best nor by reason of necessity.

In the case of the latter the existence of the effects through the causes would be by chance or unintentionally. In that case, there would be no wisdom [in creation] nor would it point to a Maker but rather to chance. For if the shape of the human hand and the number of fingers [or their magnitude][20], for instance, were not necessary or for the sake of the best in point of gripping, which is its action, or holding various things with different shapes or being useful for holding the tools of all the crafts[21], then the actions of the hand due to its shape, the number of the fingers, and their magnitude would be by chance. Were this the case, then there would be no difference whether man is endowed with a hand, a hoof or any other organ pertaining to any animal, provided it is suited to its action.

In general whenever we repudiate the causes and their effects, there remains nothing whereby the advocates of chance can be rebutted (by which I mean those who claim that there is no Maker [of this world], but that everything that happens in it is due to material causes). It is more
201 appropriate that one of two possibilities might occur by chance, than from a willing agent. Indeed, if an Ash'arite allows that the existence of one, two, or more possibilities is an indication that an agent or determinant exists, then those [advocates of chance] could rather argue that the existence of entities, according to one of two or more possibilities, is due to chance, because the will acts for a particular reason, whereas what exists for no reason or cause is due to chance. They might then argue that we see many things occurring in this way, as happens when the [four]

20. Deleted in "A".
21. In "A" *all tools of crafts*.

elements combine fortuitously in a certain way, leading to the emergence of some existing entity by chance. Then they [the elements] combine in another way by chance and thus another existing thing would emerge from that combination by chance. In this way all existing things would arise by chance.

As for us, since we hold that it is necessary that there should exist in this world such order and organization, nothing more perfect and better than which can exist, that the combinations are limited in number and are determinate, that the objects resulting from them are necessary and this never fails; it follows that it is not possible for all this to arise by chance [for what arises by chance][22] is much less necessary; in the words of the Almighty: "The handiwork of Allah who perfected everything."[23] What perfection, I wonder, would there be in existing entities if they are supposed to be merely contingent? For what is contingent is not more worthy of existence than its opposite; in the words of the Almighty: "You do not see any discrepancy in the creation of the Compassionate. So fix your gaze, do you see any cracks?"[24] What greater discrepancy could there be than that, when everything that exists could have existed with a different property, it nevertheless came to be with the one it now has? Perhaps that non-existing property is better than the existing one! Thus, whoever claims that had the easterly movement been westerly, or the westerly movement easterly, and that, in either instance, it would have

202 made no difference to the way the world was created, simply destroys the [concept of] wisdom [in creation]. He is like someone claiming that if the right of the animal were left and the left right, there would be no difference in the way the animal is made. Just as it could be said that one of two possibilities has occurred due to a free agent, who favored one of the two possibilities, it could also be said that its agent produced it in one of the two possibilities by chance, for we see that in the case of many possibilities an agent brings about one of two alternatives fortuitously.

You will no doubt recognize that all people consider that only base products could have been made differently; so that the baseness of many

22. Deleted in "B".
23. Qur'an 27: 88.
24. Qur'an 67: 3.

manufactured objects of this kind has led people to believe that they arose by chance. By contrast, they consider noble products are those that cannot be in a more perfect or complete form than the one their maker gave them. Thus, the opinion of the Mutakallimun is contrary to both religion and philosophy.

The gist of our statement that the thesis of contingency is more likely to lead to denying the existence of the Maker, rather than affirming it, besides denying Him wisdom, consists in this; that once it is held that there are no intermediates between the beginnings and the ends of products, on which the existence of these ends depends, there will be no order or organization [in this world]. And if there is no order or organization, then there would be no indication that these existing entities have a willing and knowing agent. For order, organization, and the founding of effects upon causes are the indicators that [existing entities] were produced through knowledge and wisdom. As for the existence of one possibility rather than another, it may

203 result fortuitously from an agent who is not wise. For example, a stone may fall to the ground due to its weight, to one side rather than on another, in one place rather than another, or in one position rather than another. Thus, this view leads necessarily either to denying the existence of an agent absolutely or to denying the existence of a Wise Agent, may God be Exalted and His names hallowed.

What led the Ash'arite theologians to adhere to this position was the desire to escape from recognizing the action of natural faculties which God has implanted in existing entities, endowing some with souls and other efficacious causes. They avoided admitting the existence of causes for fear of admitting that there are [in this world] active agents other than God. How can there be any other agent than God, when He is the Inventor of Causes and their causal efficacy is by His leave and His preserving them in existence? We will explain this point more fully when we discuss the issue of [divine] decree and predetermination. Further-more, they refrained from admitting natural causes for fear that they would have to admit that the world is the product of a natural cause. However, if they knew that nature is created and that there is no more conclusive proof [of the existence] of the Maker than the existence of a being so well-made, then they would have known that whoever denies nature rejects a great part of the grounds of the proof of the existence of the Maker of the world, by repudiating the existence of a part of God's creation. For, whoever repudiates one kind of existing creations denies in fact one of God's actions, which is close to denying one of His attributes.

In short since the thesis of these people is derived from provisional opinions, which are the conjectures that a person forms when he first considers an issue; and since it appears on the basis of such opinions that 204 the term "will" is predicated of whomever is capable of performing an act and its opposite, they thought that if they did not posit the existing entities as contingent, they would not be able to admit the existence of a willing Agent. Hence they claimed that all existing things are contingent, hoping to prove that the originating agent is a willing one. It is as though they failed to see that the order observed in the manufactured objects is necessary, despite the fact that it is produced by a willing Agent, who is the Maker.

Moreover, those people have failed to take into account what this position entails regarding the denial of the wisdom of the Maker and the inherence of fortuitous causation in existing things, for the things that the will produces for nothing,[25] to no end, are nothing but sheer vanity and the product of chance. Had they known, as we said previously, that, due to the presence of order in the works of nature, [existing things] must be produced by a knowing agent (otherwise the order observed in them would be fortuitous), they would not have needed to deny the actions of nature, denying thereby one contingent of God's soldiers which were enlisted by His leave, for creating and preserving many of the existing beings. For God Almighty has brought the existing things into being both by means of causes He subordinated to them from outside (namely the heavenly bodies), and causes He implanted in their very natures, which are the souls and natural powers by means of which things are preserved and wisdom fulfilled. There are none more unjust than those who deny this wisdom and impute falsehood to God.

This is the measure of the change that has occurred in this religion [of ours] concerning this and other matters that we have discussed earlier or will discuss later, God willing.

---

25. Deleted in "B".

Thus, it has become evident that the religious methods which God has laid down for His servants, whereby they might know that the world is created and made by Him, are those based on the perception of the wisdom and care for all existing entities, and especially mankind. The relation of the obviousness of this method to reason is similar to that of the sun to the senses in point of clarity.

However, the method by means of which the common people were led to comprehend this notion is through representation based on observed instances even where there are no instances of it in the visible world because the common people cannot comprehend the reality of what has no instances in the visible world. That is why the Almighty informs us that the world was created in time and that He created it from something, since nothing generated in this world is known to be otherwise. Thus He describes Himself to us prior to the generation of the world, by saying that "His Throne was upon the water"[26], and "Your Lord is truly Allah, who has created the heavens and the earth in six days, [then He sat upon the Throne]."[27] And He says: "Then He arose to heaven while it was smoke"[28]; and so on to the rest of the many verses in this vein in the Precious Book. None of these verses should be interpreted to the masses, nor should they be represented differently than the way they were represented there. Whoever alters any of that destroys the wisdom in religion.

To tell the ordinary people, however, that the religious creed, regarding the world, is that the world is created from nothing and not in time is something that the learned cannot comprehend, let alone the ordinary people. Therefore, as we said earlier, one should not diverge from the representation that religion has proposed for the ordinary people; nor should they be told otherwise, for this is the kind of representation of the creation of the world that is given in the Qur'an, the Old Testament, and other revealed Scriptures. What is really astonishing in this regard is that the kind of representation proposed by religion about the creation of the world corresponds to the notion of generation in the visible world. However, religion has refrained from expressing it in these

26. Qur'an 11: 7.
27. Qur'an 7: 54.
28. Qur'an: 41: 11.

terms because it wanted to alert the learned to the fact that the generation
206 of the world is not similar to generation in the visible world. Instead it has
used the terms "creation" and "origination"[29] as two equally suitable
terms for conveying the two notions – the generation found in the visible
world and the origination found in the invisible world – to which the
learned were led through demonstration. Therefore, the use of the terms
"creation in time" (*Ḥudūth*) and "eternity" is an innovation in religion and
a source of a great perplexity that corrupts the beliefs of the ordinary
people, and especially the dialecticians[30] among them.

That is why the greatest perplexity and worst quandary beset the
Ash'arites among the theologians of our religion. When they claimed that
God is willing with an eternal will (which is a heresy as we said earlier),
and posited that the world was created in time, they were asked: "How can
there be something willed and created in time by an eternal will?" They
answered: "The eternal will refers to creating it at a specific time, which is
the time it came to be in." But if the relation of the willing agent to the
created entity during the time in which it did not exist is the same as its
relation during the time in which it was created, then the existence of the
created entity would not have been likelier, during the time of its
existence, than during another time; unless there attached to it during its
existence a certain action which did not exist during its non-existence. If
[that relation] is not the same, then there must necessarily be a created
will, otherwise there would be a created entity from an eternal action,
since what applies with respect to the action will apply with respect to the
will. One could ask them: "If the time of the existence [of the world]
arrived, and it came to be, would it exist by an eternal action or a created
one?" If they answer "by an eternal action", then they would have allowed
the existence of a created entity from an eternal action. But if they answer
207 "by a created action", they would be forced to admit that there is a created
will. Should they say that the will is the same as the action, then they

29. *Khalq* and *Fuṭūr*. In "A", there is the addition: and initiation (*Ibtidā'*). The Almighty says:
     "Initiator of the heavens and the earth" (2: 117 and 6: 101) and "Is there any doubt about
     Allah, Maker of the heavens and the earth? (14: 10), but these are words..."Arberry translates
     the latter verse as "the Originator of the heavens and the earth".
30. The text says dialecticians, which Ibn Rushd identifies with the theologians (Mutakallimun)
     in *Faṣl al Maqāl*.

would have admitted an absurdity, because the will is the cause of the action in the willing agent. Were it possible for the willing agent to will something at a certain time, and that thing came to be when that time arrived, without any action on his part, stemming from his preceding will, then that thing could exist without an agent. Moreover, it might be thought that, if it were necessary that from a created will, a created object should arise, then from an eternal will an eternally willed object should arise also. Otherwise the object of an eternal will and that of a created will would be one and the same object, which is absurd.[31]

All these perplexities were introduced into Islam by the Mutakallimun when they divulged those religious matters that God did not permit. There is no reference in Scripture to the fact that God Almighty is willing either with a created will or with an eternal one. With respect to these matters they neither followed the literal meaning of Scripture, and thus were counted thereby among those whose happiness and salvation lie in following the literal meaning, nor did they attain the rank of the people of certainty,[32] and thus were reckoned among those whose happiness lies in the demonstrative sciences. Accordingly, they neither belong to the learned class nor the bulk of the trusting and believing class. Instead, they belong to the class of those in whose hearts there is vacillation and sickness. They admit with their tongues[33] what they deny in their hearts. The reason for this is group feeling and its love.[34] It might be that the habitual acceptance of these kinds of arguments is the reason for their abandoning rationality, as we see sometimes happen to those who have excelled in Ash'arism and practiced it since their youth. Undoubtedly those people are veiled by the veils of habit and upbringing.

What we have said so far regarding this question is sufficient for our purposes. So, let us move on to the second question.

---

31. In "A", there is the addition: "Also, how can a time be determined, while supposing an extension that has no beginning preceding it? It cannot be imagined that it is a determinate future, unless it was preceded by a determinate [past]."
32. The demonstrative class.
33. That is, verbally.
34. i.e. blind loyalty to one's group has hindered their pursuit of truth.

208 ## II. The second question: on commissioning messengers[35]

The investigation of this question revolves around two issues: one is proving [the existence of] messengers, and the other, how it can be shown that the person who claims to bear a message [from God] is really one of them and is not an imposter.

With respect to the existence of this class of people, the Mutakallimun sought to prove it syllogistically. They held that, since it has been established that God speaks, wills, and controls His servants, and since it is possible for a willing agent who controls the affairs of his servants in the visible world to send forth a messenger to those servants whom he owns, then the same thing should be possible with respect to the invisible world. They reinforced their position by rebutting the absurdities that the Brahmins attempt to infer from the existence of messengers sent forth by God.[36] [The Mutakallimun] then added that since it has been shown that [the sending off of messengers] is possible both in the invisible, as well as in the visible worlds, and since it is also evident that if, in the visible world, a person rises in the presence of the king saying: "Oh people I am the messenger of the king to you" and a sign from the king appeared to the effect that the claim of this messenger must be admitted to be true, this sign, they claimed, being the appearance of miracles at the hands of the Messenger, [he must be believed].

This is a convincing method, and in some sense is quite appropriate for the ordinary people. However, if it is examined carefully, signs of weakness will appear in it, due to what they stipulate in these principles. We do not believe the person, who claims that he is a messenger of the king, unless we know that the sign that appeared at his hand is one of those carried by the messengers of the king. This can be done either *209* through a statement of the king to his subjects, that whoever displays such a sign of my specific signs, is my messenger, or it is known that it is customary for that sign of the king not to appear except at the hands of his messengers.

---

35. Of God or apostles.
36. The Brahmins are credited in Arabic sources with denying prophethood and relying on natural reason.

If this is the case, then one might ask: "How do we know that miracles which appear at the hands of some people are signs proper to messengers?" This is known either from Scripture or reason. But it is impossible for this to be known from Scripture, since Scripture has not been ascertained yet. Neither is it possible for reason to assert that this particular sign is proper to the messengers, unless reason has already recognized repeatedly that it is a sign pertaining exclusively to certain individuals whose message is generally accepted, and did not appear at the hands of anyone else. The proof of the message must rest on two premises: first, that the person who proclaims this message has performed a miracle[37]; and second, that anyone who performs a miracle is a prophet – from which it would follow necessarily that this person is a prophet. As for the premise which states that the person professing to be a messenger has performed a miracle, it might be said that it is derived from the senses, once it is admitted that there are in fact certain actions which appear at the hands of creatures, which can be categorically asserted not to derive from some strange art or a special property, and what appears that way is not a matter of imagining.

With respect to the premise that whoever performs a miracle is a messenger, it may be granted upon the acceptance of the actual existence of messengers and the recognition that it has not appeared except at the hands of one of those whose message is found to be true. We assert that this premise is not true except in the case of one who admits the existence of the message and the existence of miracles, because this is the nature of declarative statements; the one to whom it has been demonstrated, for example, that the world is created must already know that the world exists and that [the Creator] exists as self-evident truths. If this is the case then one might raise the question: "How do we ascertain the truth of the statement that whoever performs a miracle is a messenger, when the existence of the message has not been ascertained yet – that is, assuming that we have already admitted the existence of the miracle in that manner which entails that it is miraculous?" For it is necessary that both parts of this statement – the subject and predicate – are known to exist, prior to admitting the truth of what the second asserts of the other.

210

37. Or *is one on whose hands a miracle appeared.*

It is not open for one to say that the existence of messengers is indicated by reason, on the ground that it is logically possible. For the possibility to which they[38] appeal is ignorance, which is different from that possibility which inheres in the nature of existing things; such as saying that it is possible for rain to fall or not to fall. For the possibility inherent in the nature of existing things consists in perceiving that the thing sometimes exists and sometimes ceases to exist; exactly as is the case with rain. Reason, then, judges categorically that this natural [occurrence] is possible. The necessary is the opposite of this; namely, it is that whose existence is perceived constantly, reason stipulating categorically that this nature cannot change or alter. If our opponent were to admit the existence of one single messenger at a particular time, then it would appear that the message is one
211   of those things that are possible. However, since the opponent claims that this has not been perceived yet, then the possibility that he alleges consists in the ignorance of one of two opposites; either of the possible or of the impossible. With respect to those people for whom existence of messengers is possible, [it is to be allowed that] we have admitted that possibility, because we have learned of the existence of messengers from them, unless we maintain that the perception of the existence of human messengers is evidence for the possibility of their existence, [as messengers] of the Creator, just as the existence of a messenger from *'Amr* is evidence for the possibility of his being sent by *Zayd*. This requires that the two natures are equivalent, which is very hard to accept.

However, if we assume that this is something possible in itself, albeit in the future, then it would still be a possibility only with respect to the thing in itself, but not with respect to our knowledge. Now, since one of the two opposite possibilities has come to be, it is a possibility in relation to our own knowledge; although the existence of the matter in itself is impossible on either of two opposite assumptions; that is, whether the messenger was sent or was not sent. Thus, regarding [that issue] we are ignorant, just as when we doubt whether *'Amr* has sent a messenger previously or not. This is different from raising the question: "Will he send a messenger tomorrow or will he not?" For if we were ignorant

38. The Mutakallimun.

whether *Zayd*, for example, has sent a messenger in the past or not, it would not be possible for us to judge that whoever carries a sign from *Zayd* is his messenger even if we know that this sign is that of his messenger, but only after having already known that he has actually sent a messenger. Besides all this, once we assume that the message exists and that the miraculous exists, it might still be asked: "How do we know that [he] who performs the miracle is his messenger?" For this judgment cannot be based on reported testimony, because what is based on such testimony cannot be accepted on the basis of this proposition, since it would be like correcting the thing by reference to itself,[39] which is absurd. It is not possible to appeal to experience or custom to establish the truth of this premise, unless miracles are seen to take place at the hands of messengers by those who believe in their message and, in addition, were not seen performed by others. In that case, it would be an

212 explicit sign for distinguishing the one who is a messenger sent by God from the one who is not; that is, between the one whose claim is true and the one whose claim is false. From this it can be seen that the Mutakallimun have missed the point of this aspect of the miraculous. They have substituted the possible for the existent, and discovering their ignorance of what is possible, they then tried to correct this proposition; namely, whoever is known to perform a miracle is a messenger. But [this proposition] is not true, unless the miraculous refers to the message itself and to the one who sent it. However, it is not within the power of the strange and extraordinary action that everybody regards as divine, to prove beyond doubt the existence of the message, except in so far as it is generally believed that whoever performs these things is a virtuous person, and the virtuous person does not lie. It proves that this is a messenger only if the existence of the message is admitted and this miraculous act is not the work of any other virtuous person, except a messenger. The fact is that the miraculous does not prove the validity of a message, because reason does not apprehend a relation between the two, unless it is admitted that the miraculous is one of the acts of prophethood, as healing is one of the acts of medicine. For whenever

---

39. That is, as a form of begging the question.

someone performs an act of healing, [this act] points to the existence of medicine and that [the person who heals] is a physician.

This is one of the weaknesses of this demonstration. Moreover, if we accept the existence of the Message by allowing that possibility, which is ignorance, is equivalent to existence, and regard miracle as an indication of the truthfulness of the person proclaiming the message, then it follows necessarily that [the message] will not be binding on those who believe that the miraculous might appear at the hands of someone who is not a Messenger, as the Mutakallimun do. For they allow its appearance at the hands of magicians [and at the hands of saints][40]. As for what they stipulate as a condition, that the miraculous is a proof of the message, compared with [the messenger's] proclamation of the message, and that if he were to proclaim the message, he could perform [the miraculous], 213 whereas the one who is not a messenger could not perform it; it is a claim that cannot be proved. It is not known either from reported testimony or by reason that if someone proclaims a false message, no miracles would appear at his hands. But, as we said previously, since it does not appear to be impossible that [miracles] do not appear except at the hands of virtuous people, whom God favors, and if such men were to lie, then they would not be virtuous, and the miraculous would not appear at their hands. However the persuasive force of this claim is not sufficient to convince those who allow for the appearance [of miracles] at the hands of magicians, since the magician is not a virtuous man.

This, then, is the weakness of this method, and that is why some people have held that in this case it is best to believe that miracles appear only at the hands of the prophets, and that magic is nothing but illusion that changes nothing actually. This group includes those who deny, for this reason, saintly favors (*Karamāt*).

You can see this from the lawgiver, God's blessing and prayer be upon him, who did not call anyone or any nation to believe in his message or in what he brought forth by offering in support of his message any miraculous deeds, such as turning one particular object into something else. Regarding the favors and other extraordinary deeds that appeared at

---

40. Deleted in "A".

his hands, God's blessing and peace be upon him, he performed them during his [mystical] states[41], without presenting a challenge thereby to anyone. You might ascertain this from the saying of the Almighty, "And they say: 'We will not believe you until you cause a spring to gush out from the ground for us. [Or have a garden of palms and vines; then cause the rivers therein to gush out abundantly; or cause heaven to fall upon us in fragments, as you claim; or bring Allah and the angels down, so that we can see them face to face. Or possess a house of gold, or ascend to heaven. Yet, we will not believe in your ascension, until you send down to us a book we can read.']"[42] Say: 'Glory be to my Lord; am I anything other than a human messenger?'"[43] and His saying: "Nothing prevents Us from sending the signs except that the ancients denied them."[44] The only thing 214 whereby he called people [to God] and challenged them is the Precious Book. The Almighty says: "Say: 'were men and *jinn* to band together in order to come up with the like of this Qur'an, they would never come up with the like of it, even if they back up one another.'"[45] He also says: "Come up then with ten forged *suras* like it."[46]

If this is the case, then, the extraordinary thing with which he, God's blessing and peace be upon him, challenged people and offered as evidence for his truthfulness regarding the message he proclaimed is the Precious Book.

If it is objected that although this might be obvious, one might still want to ask: "Wherefrom does it appear that the Precious Book is miraculous and that it proves that [Muḥammad] is a messenger of God, considering that you have yourself shown the tenuousness of the probative relevance of the miraculous to the existence of the message, let alone specifying the person bearing it? Besides, people have disagreed about the manner in which the Qur'an is to be considered a miracle. Some have held that it is a precondition of the miraculous that it be generically different from ordinary actions, and that the Qur'an is one of those ordinary

41. *Aḥwālih* – altered states of consciousness during periods of revelations.
42. Abridged by Ibn Rushd with the words: *up to His saying.*
43. Qur'an 17: 90–94.
44. Qur'an 17: 59.
45. Qur'an. 17: 88.
46. Qur'an 11: 13.

actions, since, according to them, it consists of words, albeit words that surpass all other contrived [human] words." They maintained, in fact, that [the Qur'an] is miraculous by virtue of deterrence – in barring people from coming up with something like it, rather than by representing a high order of eloquence. For what is of this kind differs from the ordinary in quantity rather than in kind, and things that differ only in quantity are of the same kind. Others have considered [the Qur'an] miraculous in itself and not by virtue of deterrence, without laying down the precondition that the extraordinary must be different from ordinary actions generically. They have maintained also that it is sufficient for [the miraculous] to be an ordinary action of a magnitude well beyond the capacity of all men.

We are in agreement with the objector in all this, but the matter is different from what these people[47] have imagined. The fact that the Qur'an is evidence of the truthfulness of [Muḥammad's] prophethood, 215 God's peace be upon him, rests, in our view, on two principles which the [Precious][48] Book has drawn attention to:

The first principle is that, with respect to the kind [of people], known as messengers and prophets, their existence is known in itself, and it is the kind that lays down religious laws to mankind through revelations from God and not through human learning. For no one denies their existence, except one who denies the existence of transmitted reports, such as the existence of all sorts of things that we have not seen, and famed people in wisdom, and the like. All philosophers and the rest of mankind are in agreement, except for those whose views are not worthy of consideration, that is, the naturalists (*Dahriya*), that there are, indeed, some people who receive revelations in order to inform other people about matters involving knowledge and good deeds whereby their happiness is fulfilled, and dissuade them from holding false beliefs and [committing] evil deeds. This is the [function] of the prophets.

The second principle is that anyone who is known to have promulgated religious laws through revelation from God Almighty, is a prophet. Human nature does not doubt [the truth] of this second principle. It is self-evident that the function of medicine is healing, and

47. The Mutakallimun.
48. Exists only in "S".

that whoever heals is a physician. Similarly it is self-evident that the function of the prophets, peace be upon them, is to lay down religious laws through revelation from God. Thus, whoever performs this function is a prophet.

216   As for the first principle, the Precious Book has drawn attention to it in the saying of the Almighty: "We have revealed to you as We revealed to Noah and the prophets after him. [And We revealed to Abraham, Isma'il, Isaac, Jacob and the tribes; and to Jesus, Job, Jonah, Aaron and Solomon; and We gave David a book. And [We sent forth] some apostles We have already told you about and some We have not told you about.] And Allah spoke to Moses directly."[49] The Almighty also says, "Say: 'I am not the first of the messengers.'"[50]

The second principle, namely, that Muḥammad, God's blessings and peace be upon him, has performed the function of the prophets by laying down religious laws to people through revelation from God, is known from the Precious Book. For this reason it draws attention to this principle saying, "O people, a proof from your Lord has come to you, and We sent down to you a clear light"[51] meaning the Qur'an. He also says, "O mankind, the Apostle has come to you with the truth from your Lord. If you believe, it would be better for you;"[52] and [He says] "But those firmly grounded in knowledge among men and the believers do believe in what was revealed to you and what was revealed before you." He also says: "But Allah bears witness by what He has revealed to you, that He revealed it with His knowledge. The angels bear witness too, and Allah suffices as a witness!"[53]

If someone were to ask: "How do we come to learn the first principle, which is that there is a class of people who bring down religious laws to the rest of mankind through revelation from God? Similarly, how do we come to learn the second principle that what the Qur'an contains in the form of beliefs and precepts derives from revelations from God? We

49. Qur'an 4: 163–164.
50. Qur'an 46: 9. Arberry's translation reads "Say: 'I am not an innovation among the messengers.'"
51. Qur'an 4: 174.
52. Qur'an 4: 170.
53. Qur'an 4: 166.

would answer that the first principle is learned: [1] from [the prophets] who forewarn of the things that have not come to pass yet, and then come to pass in the manner they forewarned and at the time they forewarned; [2] from the actions they have commanded; and [3] from the kinds of cognition they exhorted to, which do not resemble the cognition and actions that are learned through instruction. For what is extraordinary, when it exceeds [the kind] of knowledge involved in laying down religious laws, proves that this action is not the product of instruction, but revelation from God, and this is what is called prophethood. However, the extraordinary that does not consist in laying down religious laws, such as the splitting of the sea and the like, does not necessarily prove the property called prophethood; but only if it is conjoined to the former type of evidence. By itself this characteristic is not evidence [of prophethood]. That is why [this characteristic] does not indicate in the case of the saints

217 this notion [of prophethood], even if they have it. In this way, then, you should understand how the miraculous is a proof of prophecy. The miraculous, both in knowledge and action, is the only definitive proof of the attribute of prophethood, but the miraculous in other actions is merely a warrant and a strong proof thereof.

By now it will have become evident to you how this class of people exists and how people learn about their existence which was transmitted to us through successive reports, just as the existence of philosophers and philosophy and that of other sorts of people was transmitted to us.

If someone were to ask, "But how does the Qur'an prove that it is itself extraordinary and miraculous and of the type of miracle which indubitably proves the attribute of prophethood (extraordinary in the sense that it is intrinsic to the act of prophethood and is evidence for it, just as the act of healing is evidence for the attribute of medicine that is identical with the function of medicine)?", our answer would be that this can be learned in many ways: (1) the laws[54] contained in [the Qur'an] regarding action and knowledge cannot be acquired through instruction, but only through revelation; (2) the information it contains regarding the

---

54. *Al-Sharāʾī*, plural of *sharīʿa*. Ibn Rushd uses *Sharīʿa* to refer to religion, and sometimes to refer to religious laws. In this context, he appears to mean all the teachings of religion, including beliefs and laws.

future; and (3) its style, which differs from the style which is the product of reflection and deliberation. It is known that [the Qur'an] is of a different kind of [composition], compared to that of the eloquent speakers of Arabic, whether those who speak [Arabic] as a result of learning and art, as non-Arabs do, or native speakers like the ancient Arabs. The reference, however, is to the first way.[55]

It may further be asked: "How do we know that the religious laws, whether theoretical or practical, contained in [the Qur'an] are revealed from God Almighty, so as to deserve to be described as the word of God? 218 We would *answer* that this may be known in several ways: (1) the knowledge of the promulgating of religious laws cannot be acquired except after acquiring the knowledge of God, of human happiness, and of human misery; (2) the knowledge of voluntary matters by means of which happiness is attained, and these are goods and charitable deeds; and (3) the knowledge of those matters that impede happiness and conduce to otherworldly misery, and these are evil deeds and wickedness. The knowledge of human happiness and human misery requires the knowledge of what the self is, what its essence is, and whether it will enjoy happiness or suffer misery in the afterlife or not. If it can, then, what is the measure of that happiness and that misery? Also to what extent can the good deeds be the causes of happiness? For just as foods cannot be the cause of health in whatever amount they are consumed, and at whatever time they are taken, but rather in specific amounts and at specific times, such also is the case with respect to good and bad deeds. That is why we find all these things defined in Scriptures. Moreover, all this or most of it, does not become evident except through revelation [or is best understood through revelation][56]. Furthermore, the perfect knowledge of God is not attained, except after securing the knowledge of all the existing entities.

In addition to all this the lawgiver needs to know the measure of knowledge that would make the majority of people happy and the methods that would best lead them to this knowledge. All this, if not most of it, cannot be attained through instruction, art or philosophy. This fact may also be known with certainty by those who study the sciences,

---

55. That type not acquired through instruction.
56. Deleted in "B".

especially how to enact and determine the laws and how to teach about survival after death. Since all these matters are found in the Precious
219 Book in the most complete way possible, it must be known that this is learnt through revelation from God, and that it is the speech of God that He imparted [to mankind] on the tongue of His Prophet. For this reason the Almighty drew attention to this by saying: "Say: 'were men and *jinn* to band together in order to come up with the like of this Qur'an, they would never come up with the like of it, even if they were to back up one another.'"[57]

This matter is confirmed, or rather attains the level of decisive and complete certainty, when it is known that the Prophet, God's blessing and peace be upon him, was illiterate and was raised in an [illiterate] and common Bedouin community, who did not practice any sciences, nor were any sciences attributed to them, nor did they pursue the inquiry into existing things as the Greeks and other nations were wont to do and with whom philosophy reached its zenith over extended periods of time. There is a reference to this in the saying of the Almighty: "You did not recite before it any book or write it down with your right hand. Then the negators would have been in doubt."[58] For this reason, God praised those who worship Him for His Messenger's illiteracy in more than one verse in His Book saying: "It is He who raised up from the common nations a Messenger of their own [reciting to them His signs, purifying them and teaching them the Book and the wisdom, although they had been in manifest error before that]."[59] He also says: "[He gives life and causes to die; so believe in Allah and His Apostle,][60] the unlettered Prophet who believes in Allah and His words; and follow him, that perchance you may be well-guided."[61]

This point can be grasped in another way, namely by comparing this religion[62] with other religions. Now the function of the prophets, whereby

---

57. Qur'an 17: 88.
58. Qur'an 29: 47.
59. Qur'an 62: 2. This verse speaks of *Ummiyīn*, which could also mean illiterate or having no revealed Scripture, as against the People of the Book, or Jews and Christians.
60. Not quoted in the text.
61. Qur'an 7: 157.
62. Islam.

they are prophets, is the laying down of religious laws through revelation from God Almighty, as everybody will admit; I mean, those who believe in religious laws and in the existence of prophets, God's blessings upon them. Thus, if the Precious Book is contemplated with all the laws, which are useful both for knowledge and actions conducive to happiness it contains, and then [compared] with what all other religions and Scriptures contain, they would be found to infinitely surpass them all in this respect.

220   On the whole, if there are in some religions certain [books][63] that deserve to be called the speech of God, due to their strangeness and their departure from human modes of discourse, by virtue of what they contain of knowledge and action, then it is obvious that the Precious Book, [that is the Qur'an], is more worthy of this and deserves [to be called the speech of God] many times more than they.

You will understand this quite well, if you have perused the Old Testament and the Gospels. It is impossible for them to have all changed, and if we were to attempt to demonstrate [the superiority of one religious law over another, and the superiority of the religious law prescribed for us][64], we Muslims over the other religious law prescribed for the Jews and the Christians, as well as the superiority of the teaching proposed for us regarding the knowledge of God, the resurrection and the knowledge of the things related to them, then we would need many volumes which we admit would not suffice for such a demonstration. That is why it was said regarding this religion, that it is the seal of all religions. [The Prophet], God's peace be upon him, has said: "Had Moses lived in my time, he could not but follow me", and he was right, God's blessing and peace be upon him.

Because of the universality of the teaching of the Precious Book and the universality of the laws contained in it − by which I mean their liability to promote the happiness of all mankind − this religion is common to all mankind. That is why the Almighty says, "Say: 'Oh people, I am Allah's Messenger to you all.'"[65] [The Prophet], peace be upon him, has said, "I was sent to the red and to the black [nations]." It appears that

63. Deleted in "B".
64. In "A": *and prefer one religion of the religions revealed to us.*
65. Qur'an 7: 157.

the case of religions is similar to that of foods. Just as there are some foods that suit all people (or at least most of them), the same is true of religions. It is for this reason that all religions which have preceded ours were intended specifically for one people rather than another, whereas our religion was intended for all mankind.

In all this our Prophet, God's blessing and peace be upon him, has surpassed the other prophets because he has surpassed them in that revelation by which a prophet deserves the title of prophet. Thus, drawing attention to this distinction for which God has singled him out, he has said, God's peace upon him: "None of the prophets but I was given signs by means of which all people were called to believe. What I was given was revelation. I hope I will have the largest following on the Day of Judgment."

If all this corresponds to what we have described, then it has become evident to you that the Qur'an's proof of his prophethood,[66] God's blessing and peace be upon him, is not similar to the turning of the stick into a serpent, as a proof of the prophecy of Moses, God's peace on him, or the raising of the dead or the curing of the blind and the leper, as a proof of the prophecy of Jesus. Although these actions do not appear except at the hands of prophets and are convincing as far as the common people are concerned, they are still insufficient to prove positively, if considered in isolation, [the claim of prophethood,] since they are not actions of the type which make a prophet a prophet.

As for the Qur'an, its proof of this attribute [of prophethood] is similar to the proof of healing with respect to medicine. If two persons claimed to be physicians, and one of them said, "The proof of my being a physician is that [I can walk on water", while the other said: "The proof that I am a physician][67] is that I can heal the sick", then the former walked on water and the latter healed the sick, our recognition of the existence of medicine in the person who cured the sick would be based on demonstration, whereas our recognition of the existence of medicine in the person who walked on water would be a matter of conviction; which is a better and superior way. The kind of belief which the common people entertain in that regard rests on the notion that whoever is capable of walking on

66. Meaning the prophet Muḥammad.
67. Deleted in "A".

water, which is a superhuman feat [is more likely to be capable of healing, which is a human activity.][68] The same is true of the relation of the 222 miraculous, which is not an activity proper to the attribute [of prophethood], to the attribute whereby the prophet deserves to be a prophet; namely, revelation. To this attribute belongs what is implanted in the soul, to the effect that whomever God has empowered to perform this strange act, favoring him over all his contemporaries, has the right to claim that God has singled him out to receive His revelation.

On the whole when it has been admitted that Messengers exist and that extraordinary actions can only come from them, the miraculous becomes evidence for believing the prophet (the extraneously miraculous that is not appropriate to the attribute whereby a prophet is called a prophet that is). Perhaps the assent that results from the extraneously miraculous is the method appropriate to the common people; whereas the assent resulting from the appropriately miraculous is a method common to the common people and the learned alike. The common people are not aware of the objections and the doubts that we raised against the extraneously miraculous. However, if religion were pondered carefully, it would be found that it only takes into account the fitting and appropriate, not the extraneously miraculous.

What we have said on this subject is sufficient for our purpose and for the truth in itself.

III. The third question: on divine decree and predestination

223 This question is one of the most difficult religious questions, for if the evidence of reported testimony supporting it is examined, it is found to be conflicting, and the same is true of the evidence of rational arguments.

The conflict in the reported proofs exists both in the Book and in the orthodox Tradition (*al-Sunna*). In the Book, we find many verses that indicate that everything is predestined and that man is determined to act, and at the same time we find many verses which indicate that man earns[69] credit for his actions and that his actions are not determined.

68. Deleted in "B".
69. The noun is *kasb* or *iktisab*.

The verses indicating that everything is necessary and predetermined include the saying of the Almighty: "Indeed, We have created everything in measure,"[70] and His saying: "And everything with Him is by measure,"[71] and His saying: "Not a disaster befalls in the earth or in yourselves but is in a Book, before We created it. That for Allah is an easy matter."[72] There are many other verses indicating this notion.

However, the verses indicating that man earns credit and that existing things are contingent and not necessary, include the saying of the Almighty: "Or destroy them for what they have earned, while pardoning many,"[73] and His saying: "[Whatever calamity might hit you] is due to what your hands have earned,"[74] and His saying: "[Fear a day when you will return to Allah;] then each soul will be rewarded fully for what it has earned; [for the good works it has done] and none shall be wronged,"[75] and His saying: "But as for *Thamood*, We extended guidance to them; yet they preferred blindness to guidance."[76]

Sometimes in the same verse the conflict appears in this sense, as in the saying of the Almighty: "And when a misfortune befell you[77] after you had inflicted twice as much,[78] you said: 'Whence is this?'; say: 'It is from yourselves.'"[79] Then He says regarding this calamity itself, "And what befell you on the day the two armies met was by Allah's leave,"[80] as well as His saying: "Whatever good visits you, it is from Allah; and whatever evil befalls you, it is from yourself," and His saying: "Say, everything is from Allah."[81]

Likewise we find conflicting Prophetic traditions[82] regarding this issue, such as his saying, God's peace be on him: "Everyone is born in the state of nature (*fiṭra*), but his parents make him a Jew or a Christian"; and his

224

70. Qur'an 54: 49.
71. Qur'an 13: 8.
72. Qur'an 57: 22.
73. Qur'an 42: 34.
74. Qur'an 42: 3.
75. Qur'an 2: 286.
76. Qur'an 41: 17.
77. In the battle of *Uhud*, 625 c.e.
78. In the battle of *Badr*, 624 c.e.
79. Qur'an 3: 165.
80. Qur'an 3: 166.
81. Qur'an 4: 79.
82. *Hadith*, the collected pronouncements attributed to the Prophet.

saying: "I [Allah] made these for Paradise, and thus they perform the actions of the people of Paradise, and I made those for Hell and thus they perform the actions of the people of Hell." The first tradition indicates that the cause of unbelief is the person's upbringing, and the cause of faith is man's original nature; while the latter indicates that God creates disobedience and unbelief and that the servant's actions are predetermined.

That is why, the Muslim [community] split into two groups over this issue. One group, which is the Mu'tazilite, believed that man's "earning" is the cause of disobedience and good deeds, and it is for this reason that he is punished or rewarded. The other group, which is the Determinist[83], believed the opposite; namely, that man is predetermined in his actions and is compelled to act.

The Ash'arites, however, wanted to come up with an intermediate position between the two positions and said that, although man has the power to "earn", what he earns thereby and the act of earning are both created by God. But this is meaningless, because if God Almighty creates 225 both the power to earn and what man earns, then the servant must necessarily be determined to earn it.

This is one of the reasons for disagreement on this issue. There is a reason other than tradition for the disagreement; namely the conflicting rational proofs. For if we assume that man is the originator of his actions and their creator, then there must exist certain actions that do not occur according to God's will or His choice, in which case there will be a creator other than God. But they object that this is a [breach] of the consensus of Muslims that there is no creator other than God Almighty. However, if we assume that [man] is not free [to "earn"] his actions, then he must be compelled [to perform] them [because there is no intermediate position between determinism and earning. Then if man is compelled in his actions][84] religious obligation is intolerable[85]. For, if the human being is obliged to perform what he cannot tolerate, then there would be no difference between imposing an obligation on him and on inanimate

---

83. *Al-Jabriyah.*
84. Deleted in "B".
85. Or *unreasonable.*

objects, because inanimate objects do not have any capacity to act. Similarly man would have no capacity to do what he cannot tolerate. That is why the common people came to believe that capacity (*istiṭā'ah*) is a precondition of obligation, exactly as reason is. We find Abū al-Ma'āli[86] saying in his [treatise], *al-Niẓāmiah*,[87] that man earns his actions and he has a capacity to act, basing this on the impossibility of imposing what is intolerable, but not on the same ground precluded by the Mu'tazilites. However, the early Ash'arites permitted the imposition of what is intolerable, in an attempt to escape admitting the principle upon which the Mu'tazilites denied it – namely its being rationally abhorrent – but the [Ash'arites] disagreed with them on this point.

Moreover, if man had no power to earn, then the order to make preparations for calamities that might occur would be meaningless; and likewise [the order] to seek good things. Thus, all the arts intended to 226 bring about good things would be useless, like the art of agriculture and similar useful arts. The same applies to all the arts that aim at self-preservation and warding off harms, such as the arts of war, navigation, medicine, and the like. But all this is beyond the grasp of human reason.

It may be asked: "If this is the case, then how can one reconcile the conflict between what is based on tradition and what is based on reason?" We answer that it appears that the intention of the lawgiver is not to separate these two positions, but rather to reconcile them in an intermediate position, which is the true solution of this problem. For it seems that God, the Blessed and Exalted, has created for us faculties by means of which we can choose[88] between opposites. But since the choice of these things cannot be accomplished except through the propitiousness of the causes that God has made subservient to us from outside, and after the removal of their impediments, then the actions imputed to us occur for both reasons. If this is the case then the actions imputed to us are performed through our will, together with the propitiousness of external forces, and that is what is referred to as God's decree. These external causes that God has made subservient to us do not only complement or

---

86. Al-Juwayni, the teacher of Al-Ghazāli.
87. In "A" and "B" *inclined in the Niẓāmiah to say.*
88. Literally *earn.*

impede the actions we want to do, they are also the causes of our choice of one of the two opposites. For the will is a desire that arises in us from imagining something or from believing something. This belief is not part of our choice, but is something that arises by virtue of the things that are external to us. An example of this is that if something desirable presented itself to us from outside, we would desire it necessarily without any choice, and then we would move towards it. Similarly if something frightful descended on us from outside, we would necessarily[89] hate it and run away from it. If this is the case, then our will is preserved by the things

227 that come from outside and is bound to them. [To] this is the reference in the saying of the Almighty: "There are guardian [angels] before him and behind him, guarding him by Allah's command."[90]

However, since the eternal causes occur in accordance with a definite pattern and a well-planned order, without the slightest deviation from what their Creator has decreed for them; and since our will and our actions are not accomplished, and do not even exist, as a whole, without the concurrence of external causes, it follows that our actions occur according to a definite pattern – they take place at specific times and in a determinate measure. This must be the case because our actions are effects of these external causes. Now every effect that results from specific and determinate causes must necessarily be specific and determinate. This connection is not found between our actions and their external causes only, but also between [our actions] and the causes that God Almighty has created within our bodies. The determinate order of the internal and external causes (those that do not fail) is the decree and foreordination (*al-qaḍāʾ wa al-qadar*) that God has prescribed for His creatures; that is the Preserved Tablet.[91] God's knowledge of these causes and of what results from them is the cause of the existence of these causes. That is why no one but God encompasses the knowledge of these causes. He alone is the true knower of the Unseen, as He says: "Say: 'No one in the heavens or on the earth knows the Unseen except Allah.'"[92] The knowledge of the causes

89. In all other copies *by force*.
90. Qur'an 13: 11.
91. Or Primordial Codex, *al-lawh al-mahfouz*.
92. Qur'an 27: 65.

is tantamount to the knowledge of the Unseen, because the Unseen is the knowledge of the existence of existing entities or their non-existence in the future.

228   Now since the disposition and order of the causes call for the existence of the thing or its non-existence at a certain time, it follows that the knowledge of the causes of a certain thing is equivalent to the knowledge of the existence of that thing or its non-existence at a certain time, and the knowledge of the causes absolutely is equivalent to the knowledge of what can exist or cease to exist from them at any particular time throughout all time. How marvelous is the One who encompasses all the causes of existing entities with His inventiveness and knowledge. These are the keys of the invisible world implied in His saying, "With Him are the keys of the Unseen; only He knows them, and He knows what is on land or in the sea. [Not a leaf falls but He knows it, and there is no grain in the dark bowels of the earth, nor anything green or dry, but is [recorded] in a clear Book.]"[93]

If all this is as we have explained, then it is evident to you how we earn the merit [of our actions] and how all our earnings are foreordained. This combination is what religion has meant by those general verses and Traditions that are thought to contradict each other, but if their generality were specified in the [above] manner, their contradiction would vanish. Similarly, all the doubts urged in this regard by which I mean the conflicting rational arguments to the effect that all the things that result from our will, in fact come to be by virtue of both factors – our will and the external causes. If the actions are attributed absolutely to one of these two factors, the previously mentioned doubts will arise.

If it is said that this is a good answer in which religion agrees with reason – though it is a claim based on the assumption that there are in the world efficient causes acting on their effects, whereas the Muslim community is unanimous in the belief that there is no other agent but God – we would reply that what [the Muslim Community] has agreed

229 upon is true, but this matter admits of two responses. The first response is that what may be understood from this statement is one of two things;

93. Qur'an 6: 59.

either that there is no agent but God Almighty, or that all the other causes that He made to be subservient are not active except metaphorically; since they owe their existence to Him and it is He who caused them to exist as causes. He is indeed the one who preserves them in existence as efficacious causes and preserves their effects after coming to be. He invents their substances once their causes are conjoined to them, and He maintains them in themselves. Indeed were it not for the divine preservation these [causes and effects] would not exist for a given period of time; that is, they would not exist for the shortest period of time that can be apprehended as time. Abū Hāmid[94] says that the case of the one who makes any cause share with God Almighty the names of agent and action is similar to that of the one who makes the pen share with the writer in the act of writing; I mean by saying that the pen is a writer and the man is a writer. Thus, just as the name of writing is applied equivocally to both of them – which is to say that they are two notions which are verbally common, whereas in themselves are two very distinct things – the same is true of the name of agent when it is applied to God Almighty and to all other causes.

Our response is that there is a certain latitude in this illustration. The illustration would be obvious had the writer been the inventor of the essence of the pen and its preserver so long as it is a pen, and subsequently the preserver of the writing after it has been written and its inventor when the pen was associated with it, as we will explain later, to the effect that God Almighty is the Inventor of the substances of all the existing things that are conjoined to those causes that habit has led us to describe as their causes.

In fact this is the sense understood by senses, reason, and religion to the effect that God is the Sole Agent. The senses and reason determine that there are certain things in this world from which other things are generated and that the order pertaining to existing entities is due to two things; one is the natures and souls God has placed in them, and the other is the existing entities which surround them from outside. The most 230 important of these are the movements of the heavenly bodies. For it

94. Al-Ghazālī.

appears that [the day and the night],[95] the sun and the moon, and all the other stars are made subservient to us; and that it is due to the order and the disposition that the Creator has imparted to their movements, that our existence and the existence of whatever exists [on earth] are preserved by them; so much so that were one to imagine that one of them is removed or is imagined to be in a different position, is of a different magnitude or has a different speed from that determined by God, then all existing things on the face of the earth would perish, because of what God has instilled in their natures and instilled in the natures of things on earth, and their susceptibility to be influenced thereby. This is very evident in the case of the sun and the moon; I mean with respect to their influences on what exists herebelow. It is also evident in the case of water, the wind, the rain, the seas, and in general all sensible bodies, but their necessary existence is mostly discerned in the life of plants and many animals; indeed in all animals without exception.

Moreover, it appears that, but for the powers that God [Almighty][96] implanted in our bodies, with respect to nourishment and sensation, our bodies would have perished, as we find Galen[97] and all other philosophers admit, saying that without these powers that God implanted in the bodies of animals for their survival, it would not have been possible for the bodies of these animals to last for a single hour following their coming into being.

We hold that, but for the powers that inhere in the bodies of animals and plants, and for the forces diffused throughout the universe due to the movements of the heavenly bodies, [existing things] could not have lasted for a single moment. How marvelous is God the Subtle and the Well-informed! God has drawn attention to this in more than one verse in His Book saying: "And He subjected to you the night and the day, the sun and the moon,"[98] and in His saying, "Say: 'Have you considered, what if Allah had made the night to last, for you, continuously till the Day of Resurrection?'"[99] There is also His saying: "It was out of His mercy, that

231

95. Deleted in "A".
96. Exists only in "S".
97. Galen 129–199 C.E. (?) the most famous Greek authority in medicine in antiquity after Hippocrates 460–377 B.C.E., who is regarded as the father of medicine.
98. Qur'an 16: 12.
99. Qur'an 28: 71.

He created the day and the night, so that you may rest in it and to seek some of His bounty, [that perchance you may give thanks];"[100] and His saying: "And He subjected to you what is in the heavens and the earth all together, [as a grace] from Him,"[101] and His saying: "And He has made subservient to you the sun and the moon pursuing their courses, and subjected also the night and the day."[102] There are many other verses of this kind. If these things did not influence what exists here on earth, there would not have been any wisdom in their existence, with which He has favored us, or reckoned as one of the gifts for which we should be thankful.

The second response is that existing things consist either of substances and concrete entities or accidents like movements, heat, and cold. Substances and concrete entities cannot be invented except by the Glorious Creator. However, the causes associated with these entities affect only their accidents, not their substances. An example of this is that the sperm derives from the woman or the menstrual blood heat only; but the creation of the fetus and its soul, which is life itself, comes from God Almighty. Likewise all that the farmer does is to till the soil, fertilize it, and sow the grain in it; but the one who creates the ear of wheat is God Almighty. On this basis, then, there is no Creator but God, since in reality the existing things are the substances. To this fact the Almighty refers in saying: "O people, an example has been given; so listen to it. Surely, those whom you call upon, besides Allah, will never create a fly, even if they band together. And if a fly should rob them of something, they cannot retrieve it from them. How weak is the invoker and the invoked."[103] This also is how the unbeliever wanted to take issue with Abraham, God's peace be on him, when he said: "I give life and cause death." But when Abraham saw that [his opponent] did not
232 understand his meaning, he resorted to another argument that silenced him, saying: "Allah brings the sun from the East, bring it up from the West."[104]

100. Qur'an 28: 73.
101. Qur'an 45: 12.
102. Qur'an 14: 33.
103. Qur'an 22: 73.
104. Qur'an 2: 258.

On the whole, if the matter is understood in this way regarding the agent and the creator, no contradiction would arise with respect to tradition or that of reason. It is for this reason that we see that [the name of Creator is more appropriate to God Almighty than the name of Agent, because][105] the name of Creator is not shared between Him and the creatures, either by a near or a remote metaphor; since the meaning of Creator is the "inventor of the substances". Thus, the Almighty says: "Allah created you and what you do."[106]

You should also know that whoever denies that the causes affect their effects, with God's leave, simply repudiates wisdom and knowledge. For knowledge consists in the knowledge of existing things by means of causes, whereas wisdom is knowledge of the final causes. But the denial of the causes altogether is very alien to human nature; and those who deny the causes in the visible world do not have any means of proving the existence of an efficient cause in the invisible world, because judgment regarding the invisible world is reached by analogy with the visible world. Those people, then, have no way of knowing God Almighty, since they are forced to deny that every action has an agent. If this is the case, then from the consensus of the Muslims that there is no other agent than God Almighty should not be inferred the denial of agents in the visible world altogether. For it is from the existence of the agent [in the visible world][107], that we infer the existence of the agent in the invisible world. But once the Unseen has been confirmed for us from our knowledge of Him in Himself, we understood that everything other than He is not an agent except with His permission and by His will.

* * *

It has become evident, then, in what sense we possess "earning power" and that whoever accepts only one side of this issue, like the Mu'tazilites and 233 the Determinists, is mistaken. But the middle position that the Ash'arites wished to be the legitimate exponent of, has no basis whatsoever; since they do not allow for man any part of earning except the difference he

---

105. Deleted in "B".
106. Qur'an. 37: 96.
107. Deleted in "A".

perceives between the reflex movement of his trembling hand and the voluntary movement of his hand. Their admission of this difference is meaningless, given their claim that the two movements are not due to us. For if [these two movements] are not due to us, then we have no power to refrain from them, and accordingly we are compelled to act. Thus, the reflex movement of trembling and the [voluntary] movement that they call "earned" are the same in meaning, and thus there is really no difference between them (except verbally, and the verbal difference does not warrant a judgment regarding things themselves). All this is self-evident, so let us proceed to what is left for us of the questions we promised to deal with.

IV. The fourth question: on divine justice and injustice

234 With respect to God's justice and injustice, the Ash'arites held a very odd view from the standpoint of both reason and religion. They took a position on this issue which is not only one which was not proposed by Scripture, but also runs counter to it. They maintained that, regarding this matter, the invisible world differs from the visible world, claiming that in the visible world justice and injustice are attributed [to a person] by virtue of certain restrictions religion imposes on his actions. Thus, whenever a person performs what is considered just from the standpoint of religion, his action is just; but whoever performs an action, which religion regards as unjust, is unjust. They added that if one is not obliged or restrained by religion,[108] there will be no actions performed by him that can be described as just or unjust, so that all his actions are just. Accordingly, they committed themselves to the view that here on earth there is nothing that is just in itself or unjust in itself.

This view is of the utmost absurdity. It follows [on this view] that nothing [in the visible world] is good or bad in itself. Yet it is self-evident that justice is good and injustice bad, so that [it follows on this view] that believing that God has a partner is not unjust or wrong in itself, but only from the point of view of religion; and had religion stipulated that God

---

108. Here begins a long passage deleted in "A", which ends on p. 117 with the words "the accursed tree".

has a partner, then that would be just; and had it [stipulated] disobedience
to God, that would have been just, too. But all this is contrary to both
tradition and reason. As for tradition, God has described Himself in His
book as just and denied that He is unjust, saying: "Allah bears witness that
there is no god but He, and so do the angels and men of learning. He
upholds justice."[109] He also says: "Your Lord is not unjust to His
235 servants",[110] and "Surely, Allah does not wrong people at all; but people
wrong themselves."[111]

It might be asked: "What do you say about misguiding the servants;[112]
is it just or unjust?" There is more than one verse in His Book where God
states that He leads astray and guides rightly, such as His saying: "Then
Allah leads astray whom He pleases, and guides whom He pleases",[113] and
His saying "Had We wished, We could have granted every soul its
guidance".[114]

We answer that these verses cannot be taken at their face value.[115] For,
there are many verses which conflict with their literal meaning; such as
the verses in which the Almighty denies that He is unjust, and His saying:
"He does not approve disbelief in His servants".[116] It is evident that if He
does not approve disbelief in them, then He does not mislead them.

As for the Ash'arites' claim that it is permissible for God to do that of
which He does not approve, or enjoin that which He does not want, we
take refuge with God Almighty from this sort of belief, because it is
tantamount to disbelief.

We have evidence that people are not led astray or created in order to
err, in the words of the Almighty: "So, set your face towards religion
uprightly. It is the original nature according to which Allah has fashioned
mankind,"[117] "And [remember] when your Lord brought forth from the
loins of the children of Adam their posterity [and made them testify

---

109. Qur'an 3: 17.
110. Qur'an 41: 45.
111. Qur'an 10: 44.
112. That is, of God, or the human race.
113. Qur'an 14: 4.
114. Qur'an 32: 12.
115. Or *literally.*
116. Qur'an 39: 7.
117. Qur'an 30: 28.

against themselves. [He said]: 'Am I not your Lord?' They said: 'Yes, we testify.' [This] lest you should say on the Day of Resurrection: 'We were in fact unaware of this.']"[118] We also have the saying of the Prophet, God's blessing and peace be upon him, "Every child is born in the state of nature (*fitra*)." If in fact there is this kind of conflict [between verses of the Qur'an], then we should reconcile them in accordance with the canons of reason.

Our position is that His saying "Allah leads astray whom He pleases, and guides whom He pleases" refers to the prior [divine] will that allowed for the existence of some misguided people among the different kinds of 236 existing entities; people who are predisposed to error by their very natures and driven to it by what surrounds them of misleading causes, whether internal or external. As for His saying "Had We wished, We could have granted every soul its guidance", it means that if God had wished not to create people predisposed to being led into error, either by virtue of their own natures, of external causes or of both, He could have done so. However, since the natures of people are different, it may happen that some verses might accidentally mislead some people while rightly guiding others; not that these verses were intended to lead into error. [We find evidence of this in] His saying: "By it, He leads many astray, and guides many others rightly; but He only leads the sinners astray;"[119] and His saying: "We did not make the vision We showed you except as a trial to mankind, and likewise the accursed tree[120] in the Qur'an;"[121] and in His saying, following his enumeration of the angels of Hell: "Then Allah leads astray whom He pleases and guides whom He pleases;"[122] that is, that it might happen that the people of evil character will find these verses misleading, just as it might happen that sick bodies find nutritious foods harmful.

It might be asked: "What was the need for creating some creatures predisposed by their natures to error, and is this not the ultimate injustice?" We answer that the divine wisdom has stipulated that, so that

118. Qur'an 7: 171.
119. Qur'an 2: 26.
120. Here ends the missing paragraph in "A".
121. Qur'an 17: 60.
122. Qur'an 14: 4.

there would have been genuine injustice had matters been any different. For the nature out of which man was created and the way he was put together has necessitated that some people, or the minority, should be wicked by nature. Similarly the causes that are ordered from outside to lead people to the right path happened to be misleading to some people, while guiding the majority of people rightly. It was thus inevitable, according to the dictates of wisdom, that one of two things should happen:

237 either [God] should not create those species in which evils appear in the minority of cases, and the good in the majority, in which case the greater good would be nullified because of the lesser evil; or that He should create these species so that the greater good would coexist with the lesser evil. It is self-evident that the coexistence of the greater good with the lesser evil is better than nullifying the greater good altogether lest the lesser evil should exist. The secret of the [divine] wisdom that the angels could not grasp, as the Almighty reports [in the Qur'an] that when He told them that He was placing on earth a deputy, meaning Adam, "they said: 'Will You place one who will make mischief in it and shed blood, while we sing Your praise and glorify Your sanctity?' He said: "I know what you do not know."'[123] What [God] means is that the knowledge that was hidden from them is such that, if the existence of something is both good and evil and the good is preponderant, then wisdom stipulates its existence rather than its non-existence.

It has become evident from this discussion how leading astray is attributed to [God] along with justice and the negation of injustice. He created the causes of error because right guidance results from them more often than misguidance. For of the causes of guidance certain entities were given some [from which no error arises at all, as is the case with the angels, but other entities were given some causes of guidance that could lead][124] to error in a minority of cases. For it was not possible to instill more [guidance] in their mode of existence, due to the way they were made, and such is the case with man.

If we are asked: "What is the wisdom in the revelation of conflicting verses of this kind and forcing one to resort to interpretation, while you

123. Qur'an 2: 29.
124. Deleted in "B".

wish to exclude interpretation everywhere?" We would answer that it was due to their[125] desire to explain this matter, as it really is to the common people, that they were forced to adopt this position. For they needed to explain that God is described as Just and Creator of all things, both good and evil, because in the past many nations used to believe erroneously that there are two gods, one creating the good and the other creating evil. Accordingly they asserted that God is the Creator of both.

However, since leading astray is evil, and since there is no creator beside God, it was necessary to attribute that to Him, just as the creation of evil[126] is too. However, this must not be understood in an absolute sense because He is the Creator of the good for its own sake, and the Creator of the evil for the sake of the good; I mean, for the sake of the good that is conjoined to it. On this view, God's creation of evil could be just. An example of this is that fire was created, because it is necessary for the subsistence of many things that would not exist if fire did not exist. However, because of its nature, fire might accidentally destroy some existing things; but if we were to compare the destruction resulting from it, which is evil, and its existence, which is good, we would find that its existence is better than its non-existence, and thus it is good.

As for His saying: "He is not questioned about what He does, but they are questioned",[127] its meaning is that He does not perform any action because He is obliged to perform it; since this implies that whoever is in such a state is in need of that action, and whoever is in need of that sort of action will need it either as a matter of necessity or as a means of perfecting himself. But the Almighty Creator is above being described in this fashion. Man acts justly in order to reap what is good for him, since if he were to act unjustly, he would not reap that good. By contrast, the Almighty acts justly, not because He Himself becomes perfect through that justice, but because the perfection which is in Himself necessitates that He act justly. Thus, if this meaning is understood in that way, then it becomes clear that He is not described as just in the same sense in which the human being is so described. However, this does not imply that He

125. The Ash'arites.
126. In "A" *good*.
127. Qur'an 21: 23.

238

should not be described as just in principle, and that all the actions that emanate from Him are neither just nor unjust, as the Mutakallimun *239* imagined. For this claim destroys what is intelligible to human beings and destroys the literal meaning of Scriptures. Thus, those people groped for a certain meaning, but fell short of it. For if we assume that God cannot be described as just at all, then that will destroy what is known to reason here below to the effect that there are things that are in themselves just and good and things that are in themselves unjust and evil. Moreover, if we assume that He is characterized by being just in the same sense in which human beings are so characterized, it would follow that there is imperfection in Him. For the one who acts justly exists for the sake of that wherein he acts justly, and he is, in so far as he is just, a servant of others.

You should also know that the knowledge of this measure of interpretation is not obligatory with respect to all people, but only with respect to those who were assailed by doubts regarding this issue. However, not every common person is aware of the contradictions involved in these generalizations, so that whoever is not aware of them is obliged to accept the literal meaning of these generalizations. For there is another reason why these generalizations are given [in Scripture], which is, that [the common people] cannot conceive of the distinction between what is impossible and what is possible and God Almighty cannot be characterized as being capable of doing what is impossible. Thus, if they were told that with regard to what is impossible in itself, but possible according to them; I mean, as they imagine, that God cannot be described as capable of performing it, they would imagine that this implies imperfection and impotence in the Almighty Creator, because the one who is incapable of doing what is possible in their view is impotent. Now since the existence of all existing entities as free from evil is something possible, in the opinion of the common people, the Almighty says: "Had We wished, We would have granted every soul its guidance, but My word is now fulfilled: 'I shall fill Gehenna with *jinn* and men, all together.'"[128] However, the common people understand by this one thing, while the

128. Qur'an 32: 12.

select understand another thing; namely, that it is not incumbent on God Almighty to create people whose existence involves evil. Thus, the meaning of His saying: "Had We wished, We would have granted every soul its guidance," consists in that if He wished He would have created people whose existence involves no evil; that is, people who are purely good. In this case, every soul would be granted its guidance. This measure of explanation of this question is sufficient, so let us now turn to the fifth question.

V. The fifth question: on resurrection and its modes

240 The reality of resurrection is a matter about which all religions are in agreement and philosophers have offered demonstrative proofs. Religions, however, disagreed about the mode of this reality. In fact, they did not disagree on the mode of its existence, as much as over the representations they used to symbolize that unseen state to the common people. Some religions have described it as spiritual, pertaining to souls only, while some others have described it as pertaining to bodies and souls together. Their agreement on this point is based both on the agreement of revelation concerning that as well as the agreement of all parties regarding the necessary proofs demonstrating it. There is, then, a universal agreement that there are two kinds of happiness accessible to mankind, one is otherworldly and the other is this worldly. This agreement is based on principles acceptable to all; one of them is that mankind is nobler than most existing entities, the other is that, in so far as every existing entity appears not to have been created in vain, but rather for some function incumbent on him, which is the fruit of its existence, then man is more worthy of this function. God Almighty has drawn attention to the existence of [this matter] in all existing entities in His Precious Book saying: "We have not created the heavens and the earth and what is between them in vain. That is the presumption of the unbelievers; so woe betide the unbelievers because of the Fire."[129] He has also praised the scholars who recognized the purpose incumbent on this existence saying: "Those who remember Allah while standing, sitting or lying on

129. Qur'an 38: 27.

their sides, reflecting upon the creation of the heavens and the earth [saying]: 'Our Lord You did not create this in vain. Glory be to You! Save us from the torment of the Fire.'"[130] For the existence of the purpose in [the creation of] man is more evident than in all other existing entities. The Almighty has drawn attention to it in more than one verse in His book, saying: "Did you, then, think that We created you in vain and that unto Us you will not be returned?"[131] and "Does man think that he shall be left unattended?"[132] and "I have not created *jinn* and mankind except to worship me",[133] meaning the kind of beings who know Him. Drawing attention to the rise of the obligation to worship consequent to knowing the Creator, He also says: "And why should I not worship Him who created me and unto Him you shall be returned."[134]

241

Thus, if it appears that man is created for certain functions intended for him, then it becomes clear that these functions must be peculiar [to him]. For we see that each one of the existing entities is created for the sake of the particular function that belongs to it rather than to something else, (I mean, that which is peculiar to it). Now if this is the case, then the purpose of mankind must consist of those activities that are peculiar to them, as distinct from all other animals, and these are the activities of the rational self. However, since the rational self has two parts, one theoretical and the other practical, it follows that what is required primarily from him is to be perfect with respect to these two powers, the practical and theoretical virtues, and that the actions that enable the soul to acquire these two types of virtue are the good things and good deeds; whereas those that impede it are the evil things and bad deeds.

Now since the determination of these actions derives mostly from revelation, the various Scriptures undertook to determine them, as well as define them and exhort people to perform them. Thus, they commanded the pursuit of virtues and prohibited the vices, determining the exact measure in which the happiness of the whole of mankind consists, in point of both theory and practice; I mean, the happiness common to mankind.

130. Qur'an 3: 191.
131. Qur'an 23: 115.
132. Qur'an 75: 36.
133. Qur'an 51: 56.
134. Qur'an 36: 21.

Thus, with respect to speculative matters, they defined the part which all people should know, which is the knowledge of God, Most High, the knowledge of the angels and of other noble entities, and the knowledge of happiness. Likewise, they defined the measure of actions whereby human souls are virtuous in the practical sense; especially this our religion. 242 Indeed, if it is compared to all other religions, it would be found to be absolutely the most perfect religion; and that is why it is regarded as the final religion.

Now, in all religions revelation has warned that the soul is imperishable, and the philosophers have offered demonstrative proofs of that [imperishability]. Moreover, human souls are rid after death of bodily appetites, [and if they are pure, their purity is doubled upon being freed from bodily appetites],[135] but if they are wicked, their separation from the body will make them still more wicked because they are injured by the vices that they had earned, and their distress at the loss of that purity which they missed will increase upon leaving the body; since that missed purity cannot be acquired except in conjunction with the body. To this state is the reference in the saying of the Almighty: "Lest any soul should say: 'Woe betide me for what I have neglected of my duty to [Allah and for having been one of the scoffers].'"[136] Accordingly all religions have concurred in making this condition known to people and calling it ultimate happiness or ultimate misery.

However, since there is nothing akin to this state in the seen world to compare it with, and since the measure of what is known of it through revelation differs from one prophet to another, because the [prophets] differ from one another in this respect (I mean, on the question of revelation), religions have differed in their representations of the states of the happy and the miserable souls after death. Some of them have refrained from representing the pleasures that are in store for the pure souls and the pains for the miserable ones in visible forms, declaring that all these states are spiritual states and angelic pleasures. By contrast, other religions have resorted in representing these states to invisible forms, assimilating the pleasures attainable in [the afterlife] with pleasures

135. Deleted in "B".
136. Qur'an 39: 56, the sentence between the brackets is deleted in "A".

attainable here below, after discounting any harm that might be associated with [such worldly pleasures]. They assimilated the pain experienced in 243 the afterlife to the pain that is experienced here below, after dissociating it from any abatement that might attend it in this world. The reason why the founders of these religions [resorted to this kind of assimilation] is either that they knew, through revelation, aspects of these states that were not known to those who represented them spiritually, or deemed that representing them by reference to sensible matters is more effective in leading the common people to understand; since they are more likely to be drawn or repelled by them respectively. Thus, [the prophets] informed us that God restored the happy souls to bodies in which they will eternally partake of the most enjoyable sensual pleasures, such as in Paradise; and that contrariwise, He restores the wicked souls to bodies in which they will suffer for all time the most painful of sensual experiences, such as in hellfire.

This is the procedure of our own religion which is Islam, in representing the hereafter. Our Precious Book offers many general proofs accessible to everybody, regarding the possible existence of these states, since the human intellect cannot conceive, when it attends to these matters, more than the mere possibility that is open to the common apprehension of everyone. All this is a matter of analogy of the existence of what is equal to the existence of its equal in its coming into being, that is, and, of comparing the possibility of existence of the more or less to the coming into being of the greater and the smaller as in God's saying: "And he produced an equal for us, forgetting Our creating him. [He said: 'who brings the bones back to life, once they are withered?']"[137] The argument implied in these verses consists in drawing an analogy between restoration and origination, which are equal. There is in this verse, in addition to the analogy, which confirms the possibility of the restoration, a rebuttal of the rejection by the opponent of this view, by reference to the difference between origination and restoration, as in the saying of the Almighty: "Is it not He who produces fire from green trees for you?"[138] The objection is that the origination was due to heat and moisture and the restoration to

137. Qur'an 36: 78.
138. Qur'an 36: 80.

cold and dryness, and thus it was countered by asserting that we perceive that God Almighty brings forth the opposite from its opposite by creating one from the other, just as He creates the like from its like. As for the analogy of the possibility of the existence of the less to the existence of the 244 more, we have the saying of the Almighty: "Is not He who created the heavens and the earth able, then, to create the like of them? Yes indeed, and He is the All-knowing Creator."[139] These verses contain two proofs of the resurrection and a refutation of the argument of those who deny it. However, if we were to enumerate the verses in the Precious Book containing these proofs, we would be guilty of prolixity, since they are all of the same type we have described.

Thus, as we stated earlier, all the different religions are in agreement that souls experience, after death, certain states of happiness and suffering; but they disagree in the manner of representing these states and in explaining the mode of their existence to mankind. It appears that the way our religion represents them is more adequate for making the majority of people understand them and rendering their souls more eager to seek what exists [beyond this life]. After all, the primary target [of religions] is the majority [of people]. It appears that the spiritual representation is less effective in stimulating the souls of the common people to [seek] what lies beyond, and the common people are less desirous and less fearful of it than they are of corporeal representations. [For this reason the corporeal representation seems][140] to be a stronger impetus for seeking the hereafter than spiritual representation, and the spiritual is more acceptable to the dialectical theologians, who are in the minority.

For this reason we find the people of Islam divided, regarding the understanding of that representation of the states of resurrection that our religion proposes, into three sects:

One sect holds that life after death is exactly the same as this life, with respect to bliss and pleasure; that is, they believe that the two are of the same kind, differing only in the manner of their duration and cessation, the former being permanent, while the latter ephemeral.

139. Qur'an 36: 80.
140. Deleted in "B".

Another group holds that the two modes of existence are distinct, and this group has splintered into two. The first believes that the existence depicted in these sensual representations is spiritual, but it was 245 represented in that way for stylistic reasons. This [group] has appealed to many other religious arguments, which we need not enumerate here.

A third group believes that [resurrection] is corporeal, but that the corporeality that exists in the afterlife differs from corporeality in this life, because the former is everlasting while the latter is ephemeral. This group has a series of religious arguments, too. Ibn Abbas[141] seems to belong to the latter group, for he is reported as saying, "Nothing in this world is analogous to the next one, except the names." It is likely that this view is more appropriate for the elect, since it is founded on facts uncontested by anyone. One of these is that the soul is immortal, and the other is that the return of the soul to different bodies does not involve the absurdity that the supposition of the return of the same bodies involves. For it appears that the material components of bodies in this world exist in succession and are transmitted from one body to another; that is, the same matter supervenes on many persons at different times. But it is impossible for the 246 likes of all these bodies to exist in actuality because they are made of the same matter. For example, a person dies and his body turns to earth, then the earth is transformed into plants on which some other person feeds and from his semen another man is generated. However, if different bodies are assumed to exist [in the hereafter], then no such absurdity would arise.

The truth of the matter is that the obligation incumbent on each person is to take the position to which his speculation leads him to; provided that such speculation does not completely destroy the original principle; namely, the denial of the existence [of life after death] altogether. This kind of belief necessitates that its holder be declared an unbeliever, because the knowledge of the existence of this state of man [after death] is known to all people through religion and reason. All this is based on the immortality of the soul.[142]

---

141. The Prophet's uncle and an authority on the transmission of Prophetic traditions (*Hadiths*).
142. In "A" there is the addition: "But the thoughts of the general public are not moved to correct these conceptions of the resurrection, but they are moved to follow the Scriptures and practice the virtues."

If it is asked: "Does religion have any proof for the immortality of the soul or any indication of it?", we would answer that all that is found in the Precious Book, where the Almighty says: "Allah carries off the souls of men upon their death and the souls of those who are not dead in their sleep. [He then holds back those whose death He has decreed and releases the others till an appointed time. Surely, there are in that signs for people who reflect.]"[143] The point of the proof in this verse is that He equates sleeping with death in suspending the activity of the soul. Were the suspension of the activity of the soul at death due to its corruption, and not for the change of its instrument,[144] then the suspension of its activity during sleep should have been due to its corruptibility, too. However, were this the case, then it would not return upon awakening to its own state. For since it returns to its own state we know that the suspension of its activity does not happen to it due to a defect in its essence, but is the 247 result of some deficiency affecting its instrument. Hence, it does not follow that if the instrument is corrupted, the soul must be corrupted, too. Death is a form of corruption; therefore it should affect the instrument, as happens during sleep; or as the Philosopher says: "If the old man were to find an eye like the young man's eye, he would be able to see as well as the young man sees."[145]

This is what we thought should be stated in the exposition of the beliefs of this our community, which is the community of Islam.

---

143. Qur'an 39: 42.
144. Meaning the body.
145. Aristotle, *De Anima*, i, 4, 408b 21.

Conclusion: the canon of
interpretation

Of the questions we promised it remains for us to discuss which parts of religion are, and which parts are not, susceptible of interpretation; and regarding what is so susceptible, who is entitled to undertake it? With this discussion, we will conclude this book.

Our position is that there are five levels of meaning in religion. These levels are divisible, in the first instance, into two major types. The first is indivisible, and the second is divisible into four different types.

The first indivisible type consists in that the declared meaning is identical with the real meaning.

The second divisible type consists in that the declared meaning in Scripture is other than the real meaning; but is substituted for it by way of representation.

The latter type is divided into four parts. The first is that whose representation is given [in Scripture], but whose existence is only known through lengthy and complex syllogisms that are learnt over a long period of time and through various arts and are not understood except by people of superior natures. Besides, it is not possible to know that the given representation is other than what is represented, except through the lengthy process we mentioned.

The second part is the opposite of the [first]. Here the two cases¹ are

1. The Scriptural term and its interpretation.

known relatively easily; I mean, that that declared [by Scripture] to be a representation is a representation and the reason why it is a representation.

249   The third part is when it is known readily to be a representation of the thing in question and why, in an elaborate way.

The fourth is the opposite of this, where it is known readily *why* it is a representation, but with difficulty *that* it is a representation.[2]

As for the first type of the two divisions, it is undoubtedly an error to interpret it.

With respect to the first type of the second division, which is the result of elaborate study in both respects[3], its interpretation is confined to those well-grounded in knowledge, and it is not permissible to divulge it to those not well-grounded.

However, with respect to the opposite type, where both cases are readily grasped, its interpretation is meant and divulging it is obligatory.

[With respect to the third type, the matter is different.][4] Representation is not attempted here [because it is beyond the understanding of the common people, yet this representation is attempted][5] so as to move the souls towards it. This is similar to the saying of the [Prophet], peace be on him: "The Black Stone is God's right hand on earth", to which may be added other similar sayings which are either self-evident or readily known to be representations, but are known through an elaborate process why they are representations. The obligation in this case is not to be interpreted except by the elect among the learned. Those who know that this is a representation, but do not belong to men of learning, will be told why it is a representation; either because it is ambiguous [that is known by those well-grounded in knowledge][6], or because the representation thereof is reduced to what is closer to their understandings. Perhaps this is the proper course in order to dispel the lingering ambiguity in their souls from that. The rule to follow in this type of speculation is the one Abū

2. Translator's italics.
3. That is, both what is declared as a representation and the reason why it is a representation.
4. Deleted in "S".
5. Deleted in "A".
6. This part is smudged in "S".

Hāmid [Al-Ghazāli] adopted in *The Book of the Distinction*.[7] Here this class is informed that the same thing admits of five modes of existence: the essential, the sensible, the imaginary, the intelligible, and the ambiguous, as Abū Hāmid [al-Ghazāli] calls them. Thus, when a problem arises, one considers which of the four modes of existence is more convincing for that class of people who find it impossible that such statements could denote the essential existence (the one that is external[8]). Representation should, then, be couched in terms of the mode of existence that they believe is most likely to exist. To this type, the saying of [the Prophet], peace be upon him, actually refers: "There is nothing that I have not seen but I have seen it already in this station of mine, even Paradise and Hell";[9] his saying: "Between my basin and my pulpit there is one of the gardens of Paradise, and my pulpit is by my basin";[10] and his saying "Dust will consume every son of Adam except the *coccyx of the tail*".[11] All these are readily known to be representations, but it cannot be known why they are representations except through elaborate knowledge. Thus, it should be assigned to that class of people who have understood readily the similarity of the four modes of existence. If this kind of interpretation is used in these contexts and in this way, then its use in religion is permissible; but if it is used in other contexts, then it is wrong. Abū Hāmid [al-Ghazāli], however, did not discuss this issue in detail, as when, for instance, the context lends itself to knowing both aspects of the problem in an elaborate way; I mean, that it is a representation and why it is a representation. In that case, an ambiguity might arise giving, at first sight, the impression that it is a representation; but this is a false ambiguity. The obligation in this case is to ignore that ambiguity and no interpretation be attempted, as we have shown you in this book in the many places where the Mutakallimun, I mean, the Ash'arites and the Mu'tazilites were faced with this [ambiguity].

However, the fourth type, which is the opposite of this, consists in the fact that its being a representation is known in an elaborate way. But if it is

7. *Distinction between Islam and Heresy (al-Tafriqa bayna al-Islām wal-Zandaqah)*.
8. Or *concrete*.
9. Wensinck, *Concordance*, s.v. *ra'a*. Bukhari, iii, 24.
10. Wensinck, *Concordance*, s.v. *hawd*. Bukhari, xx, 5.
11. Muslim, *Fitn*, 142.

admitted to be a representation, and it can readily be known why it is a representation, then its interpretation is open to question (I mean, with respect to that class of people who perceive that if it is a representation, then why; but they do not perceive that it is a representation, except in an ambiguous manner and a persuasive way, since they do not belong to those well-grounded in knowledge). Thus, it might be said that it is safer
251 for religion that these matters should not be interpreted, lest those people cease to believe the things for which they took that statement to be a representation, and is rather the most likely. It might also be possible to allow them free rein to practice interpretation, on account of the strong similarity between that thing and that whereby it is represented. However, once interpretation is allowed in these two cases, many strange beliefs are generated therefrom that are very remote from the literal meaning of Scripture. They might become widespread and the common people would reject them, as happened to the Sufis and to those scholars who followed their lead.

* * *

Thus when control over interpretation passed to those who could not discriminate between these contexts, nor determine the class of people to whom it is permissible to engage in the interpretations, confusion arose, with respect to these matters, and many divergent sects arose accusing each other of unbelief. All this is tantamount to ignorance of the intent of the Scripture and a violation thereof. However, you have no doubt perceived from our discussion the extent of error that results from [false] interpretations. It is my sincere wish to be able to achieve this goal [of interpretation] regarding all the statements of Scripture – to discuss what ought or what ought not to be interpreted, and if it is to be interpreted, then who should interpret it – with respect to all problematic issues in the Qur'an and the *Hadith*, reducing them all to these four categories [mentioned above].

* * *

Now the purpose that we set for ourselves in this book has been accomplished. We proposed it because we felt that it was the most important goal pertaining to religion. It is God who guides to the truth and guarantees the reward with His grace and mercy. This book was finished in the year five hundred and seventy-five.[12]

---

12. 575 of the *Hijra* Calendar or 1179/80 C.E.

Selected Bibliography

Açikgenç, Alparslan. "Ibn Rushd, Kant and Transcendent Rationality: A Critical-Synthesis", *Alif*, 16 (1996), 164–190

Al-Iraqi, Atif. *Al-Manhaj al-Naqdy fi Falsafat Ibn Rushd*, Cairo, Dar al-Ma'ārif, 1980

Al-Iraqi, Atif. *Al-Naz'a al-'Aqlia fi Falsafat Ibn Rushd*, Cairo, Dar al-Ma'ārif, 1993

Al-Iraqi, Atif. *Thawrat al-'Aql fi al-Falsafat al-'Arabiya*, Cairo, Dar al-Ma'ārif, 1993

Al-Mousawi, Mousa. *Mina al-Kindi ila Ibn Rushd*, Beirut, Uwaydat, 1982

Al-Ubeidy, Hamady. *Ibn Rushd wa Ulūm al-Shari'ā al-Islamia*, Beirut, Dar al-Fikr al-Arabi, 1991

Amin, Uthman. *Ibn Rushd, Talkhis [Jawami] Ma Ba'd al-'Tabi'a*, Cairo, Mustafa al-Halabi wa-Awladuhu, 1958

Ammara. "Al-Mawqif min al-Turath al-'Aqlani li-Ibn Rushd", *Al-katib* (August, 1973), 80–100

Ammara. "Ibn Rushd wa-'al-Falsafa al-'Aqliyya fi al-Islam", *Al-Tali'a.* (November, 1968), 135–153

Antoun, Farah. *Ibn Rushd wa Falsafatuhu*, Beirut, Dar al-Farabi, 1988

Arberry, A.J. *Aspects of Islamic Civilization.* Ann Arbor, University of Michigan Press, 1971

Atiyya Ahmad Abdul-Halim. "Ibn Rushd on the Question of Women: Preliminary Remarks", *Alif* 16 (1996), 145–16

Averroes. *Commentary on Plato's 'Republic'.* Erwin Rosenthal (ed., trans. and int.) Cambridge, University of Cambridge Oriental-Publications/Cambridge University Press, 1956

Averroes on the Harmony of Religion and Philosophy. (London, Luzac & Co., for E.J.W. Gibb Memorial Series and UNESCO, 1961) A translation of Fasl al-Maqal with introduction and notes by George F. Hourani

Averroes. *The Incoherence of the Incoherence* [*Tahāfut al-Tahāfut*], translated from the Arabic with an introduction and notes by Simon Von Den Bergh, printed Oxford, Oxford University Press, for the Trustees of the E.J.W. Gibb Memorial and published by Messrs. Luzac & Co., 1954

Baisar, Muhammad 'Abd al-Rahman. *Fi Falsafat Ibn Rushd, al-Wujūd wa-'l-Khulūd*, 3rd edn. Beirut, Dar al-Kitab al-Lubnani, 1973

Butterworth, Charles (ed.). "Averroes, Precursor of the Enlightenment?" *Alif* 16 (1996), 6–18

Butterworth, Charles (ed.). *Averroes' Three Commentaries on Aristotle's "Topics", "Rhetorics", and "Poetics",* Albany, State University of New York Press, 1971

Butterworth, Charles E. and Blake A. Kessel (eds.). *The Introduction of Arabic Philosophy into Europe,* Leiden, New York, Köln, E.J. Brill, 1994

Butterworth, Charles E. (ed.). *The Political Aspects of Islamic Philosophy: Essays in Honor of Muhsin Mahdi,* distributed for the Center for Middle Eastern Studies of Harvard University by Harvard University Press, Cambridge, Massachusetts, 1992

Corbin, H. *Histoire de la philosophie islamique,* Paris, Gallimard, 1964

Craig, William L. *The Kalam Cosmological Argument,* New York, Harper and Row, 1979

Cropsey, Joseph (ed.). *Ancients and Moderns: Essays on the Tradition of Political Philosophy in Honor of Leo Strauss,* New York and London, Basic Books, 1964

Davidson, Herbert A. *Alfarabi, Avicenna, and Averroes on Intellect: Their Cosmologies, Theories of the Active Intellect, and Theories of Human Intellect.* New York, Oxford University Press, 1992

De Boer, T.J. *Geschichte der Philosophie im Islam,* Stuttgart, F. Frommanns Verlag, 1901; trans. as *The History of Philosophy in Islam,* E.R. Jones, London, Luzac, 1903)

El-Khodeiry, Zeinab Mahmoud. "Ibn Rushd Between Pluralism and Oneness", *Alif* 16 (1996), 36–51

Fakhry, Majid. *A History of Islamic Philosophy,* 2nd edn, New York, Columbia University Press, 1983

Fakhry, Majid. *Ibn Rushd: Faylasuf Qūrtuba,* Beirut, Catholic Press, 1960

Fakhry, Majid. *Islamic Occasionalism and its Critique by Averroes and Aquinas,* London, Allen & Unwin, 1958

Gauthier, L. *Ibn Roshd (Averroes)*, Paris, Presses Universitaires de France, 1948

Gauthier, L. *La Thóorie d'Ibn Roshd (Averroes) sur les Rapports de la Réligion et de la Philosophie*, Paris, Lerous, 1909

Gibb, H.A.R. *Modern Trends in Islam*, Chicago, University of Chicago Press, 1947

Hackett, Jeremiah. "Averroes and Roger Bacon on the Harmony of Religion and Philosophy" in Ruth Link-Salinger (ed.), *A Straight Path: Studies in Medieval Philosophy and Culture*, Washington, D.C., Catholic University of America Press, 1988, 98–112.

Hanafi, Hassan. "Ibn Rushd as a Jurist", *Alif* 16 (1996), 116–144

Hanafi, Hassan. "Ibn Rushd Sharihu Aristu", proceedings of *Mu'tamar Ibn Rushd: al-Dhikra Al-Mi'awiyya al-Thamina li-Wafatihi* (4–9 Nov. 1978) in Algiers, al-Mu'assasa al-Wataniyya li-al-Funun al-Matba'iyya, 1985/86, 57–120

Hernandez, M.C. *Ibn Rushd (Averroes)*, London, 1997

Hourani, George (ed.). *Essays on Islamic Philosophy of Science*, Albany, State University of New York Press, 1975

Hourani, George (ed.). *Kitab Faṣl al-Maqāl*, Leiden, E.J. Brill, 1959

Ibn Rushd. *Talkhis Mantiq Aristu*, Vol. 1 *(al-Qiyas)*, Beirut, Lebanese University Press, 1982

Ibn Rushd. *Al-Kashf 'an Manāhij al-Adilla fi 'Akai'd al-Milla*, 2nd edn. Ed. Mahmud Qasim. Cairo, al-Maktaba al-Anglo al-Misriyat, 1964

Ibn Rushd. *Al-Kashf 'an Manāhij al-Adilla fi 'Akaid al-Milla*. Ed. Muhammad 'Abid Al Jabiri, Beirut, Markaz Dirāsāt al-Wahda al-'Arabia, 1998

Ibn Rushd. *Bidāyat al-mūjtahid wa-nihāyat al-mūqtasid*, two volumes, Cairo, Dar al-Hamami li al-Tiba'a, 1975

Ibn Rushd. *Kitab al-Būrhan*, Cairo, American Center for Research, 1980

Ibn Rushd. *Tahāfut al-Tahāfut*, Beirut, Dar al-Fikr al-Lubnani, 1993

Ivry, Alfred L. "Averroes and the West: The First Encounter/Non-Encounter", in Ruth Link-Salinger, (ed.), *A Straight Path: Studies in Medieval Philosophy and Culture*, Washington D.C., Catholic University of America Press, 1988, 142–58

Kogan, B.S. *Averroes and the Metaphysics of Causation*, New York, State University of New York Press, 1985

Kogan, Barry S. "Averroes and the Theory of Emanation", *Mediaeval Studies*, 43 (1981), 384–404.

Leaman, Oliver. *Averroes and his Philosophy*, Oxford, Clarendon Press, 1988

Mabrook, Ali. "The Evasive Defeat of Rationalism: From Ibn Rushd to Ibn Khaldoun", *Alif* 16 (1996) 89–115

Mahdi, Muhsen. "Averroes on Divine Law and Human Wisdom", in Joseph Cropsey (ed.). *Ancients and Moderns, Essays on the Tradition of Political Philosophy in Honor of Leo Strauss.* New York, Basic Books, 1964, 114–131

Mahdi, Muhsen. "Remarks on Averroes' Decisive Treatise". in Michael E. Marmura (ed.). *Islamic Theology and Philosophy: Studies in Honor of George F. Hourani,* Albany, State University of New York Press, 1984 188–202, 305–308

Mahdi, Muhsin. "Review of George F. Hourani, ed., Ibn Rushd (Averroes): Kitab Fasl al-Maqal, with Its Appendix (Damima) and an Extract from Kitab al-Kashf an Manahij al-Adilla", *Journal of Near Eastern Studies* 21 (1961), 149–170

Mahdi, Muhsin. "On Ibn Rushd's Philosophy and the Arab World (interview)", *Alif,* 16 (1996), 255–258

Marakushi, M. *Al-Mu'jib fi Akhbār al-Maghrib,* Leiden, 1885

Marmura, M.E. (ed.). *Islamic Theology and Philosophy: Studies in Honor of George F. Hourani.* Albany, State University of New York Press, 1984

Mesbahi, Mohamed. "The Right to First Principles between Philosophy and Science according to Ibn Rushd", *Alif* 16 (1996), 52–76

Morewedge, P. (ed.). *Islamic Philosophy and Mysticism.* Delmar, New York, Caravan Books, 1981

Munk, S. *Mélanges des philosophie juive et arabe,* A. Franck, Paris, 1859

Musa, Muhammad Yusuf. *Ibn Rushd al-Failasuf.* Cairo, Dar Ihya al-kutub al-'Arabiyya, 1945

Najjar, Ibrahim Y. "Ibn Rushd's Theory of Rationality", *Alif* 16 (1996), 191–216.

Nasr, Seyyed Hossein and Oliver Leaman (eds.). *History of Islamic Philosophy,* London and New York, Routledge, 1996

Qasim, Mahmud. *Ibn Rushd: al-Faylasuf al-Muftara Alayhi,* Egypt, Maktabat al-Anglo al-Misriyat, n.d.

Qasim, Mahmud. *Nazariat al-Marifat inda Ibn Rushd.* Egypt, Maktabat al-Anglo al-Misriyat, n.d.

Renan, E. *Averroes et l'averroîsme,* Paris, 1882

Rosenthal, Erwin. *Political Thought in Medieval Islam.* Cambridge, Cambridge University Press, 1958

Rosenthal Erwin, (ed., trans. and int.) *Averroes' Commentary on Plato's 'Republic'.* Cambridge, University of Cambridge Oriental-Publications/Cambridge University Press, 1956

Salim, Muhammad Salim (ed.). *Ibn Rushd, Talkhis al-khataba.* Cairo, al-Majlis al-A'la li-'l Shu'un al-Islamiyya, 1967

Schaub, Mark. "Rhetorical Studies in America: The Place of Averroes and the Medieval-Arab Commentators", *Alif* 16 (1996), 233–254.

Sharif, M.M. (ed.). *History of Muslim Philosophy*, Wiesbaden, Harrassowitz, 1963–66

Stelzer, Steffen. "Decisive Meetings: Ibn Rushd, Ibn 'Arabi, and the Matter of Knowledge", *Alif* 16 (1996), 19–55

Tizani, Tayyib. "Ibn Rushd-Qimmat al-Fikr al-Maddi al-Aqlani al-Wasit; Talashi al-Thunā'iyya baina al-'Alam wa-'l-Ilāh" in *Mashru' Ru'ya Jadida li-al-Fikr al-'Arabi fi al-'asr al-Wasīt*, Damascus, Dar Dimashq, 1971, 355–388

Urvoy, Dominique. *Ibn Rushd (Averroes)*, Cairo, The American University in Cairo Press, 1991

Von Kügelgen, Anke. "A Call for Rationalism: Arab Averroists in the Twentieth Century", *Alif* 16 (1996), 97–132

Watt, M. *Islamic Philosophy and Theology*, Edinburgh, Edinburgh University Press, 1962

Wolfson, Harry A. *The Philosophy of the Kalam*, Cambridge, Massachusetts, Harvard University Press, 1976

Index of Qur'anic Verses

Note: references appear in the following form: verse number, verse line, Arabic verse name, English verse name, page number.

Index